SKILLS MASTERY

This Book Includes:

- Practice questions to help students master topics assessed on the PARCC and Smarter Balanced Tests.
  - Reading: Literature
  - Reading: Informational Text
  - Language
- Detailed Answer explanations for every question
- Strategies for building speed and accuracy
- Content aligned with the Common Core State Standards

Plus access to Online Workbooks which include:

- Hundreds of practice questions
- Self-paced learning and personalized score reports
- Instant feedback after completion of the workbook

Complement Classroom Learning All Year

Using the Lumos Study Program, parents and teachers can reinforce the classroom learning experience for children. It creates a collaborative learning platform for students, teachers and parents.

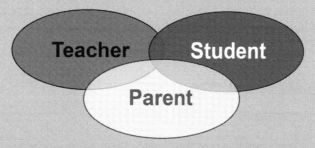

Used in Schools and Libraries
To Improve Student Achievement

Lumos Learning
Developed by Expert Teachers

Common Core Practice - 6th Grade English Language Arts: Workbooks to Prepare for the PARCC or Smarter Balanced Test

Contributing Author	-	**Heather D.**
Contributing Author	-	**Janet Redell**
Contributing Author	-	**Marisa Adams**
Executive Producer	-	**Mukunda Krishnaswamy**
Designer	-	**Raghavendra Rao R.**

ISBN-10: 1940484529

ISBN-13: 978-1-940484-52-5

Printed in the United States of America

For permissions and additional information contact us

Lumos Information Services, LLC
PO Box 1575, Piscataway, NJ 08855-1575
http://www.LumosLearning.com

Email: support@lumoslearning.com
Tel: (732) 384-0146
Fax: (866) 283-6471

Developed by Expert Teachers

Table of Contents

Introduction

The Common Core State Standards Initiative (CCSS) was created from the need to have more robust and rigorous guidelines, which could be standardized from state to state. These guidelines create a learning environment where students will be able to graduate high school with all skills necessary to be active and successful members of society, whether they take a role in the workforce or in some sort of post-secondary education.

Once the CCSS were fully developed and implemented, it became necessary to devise a way to ensure they were assessed appropriately. To this end, states adopting the CCSS have joined one of two consortia, either PARCC or Smarter Balanced.

Why Practice by Standard?

Each standard, and substandard, in the CCSS has its own specific content. Taking the time to study and practice each one individually can help students more adequately understand the CCSS for their particular grade level. Additionally, students have individual strengths and weaknesses. Being able to practice content by standard allows them the ability to more deeply understand each standard and be able to work to strengthen academic weaknesses.

Why Practice with Repeated Reading Passages?

Throughout the Lumos Learning Common Core Practice workbooks, students and educators will notice many passages repeat. This is done intentionally. The goal of these workbooks is to help students practice skills necessary to be successful in class and on standardized tests. One of the most critical components to that success is the ability to read and comprehend passages. To that end, reading fluency must be strengthened. According to Hasbrouck and Tindal (2006), "Helping our students become fluent readers is absolutely critical for proficient and motivated reading" (p. 642). And, Nichols et al. indicate, (2009), "fluency is a gateway to comprehension that enables students to move from being word decoders to passage comprehenders" (p. 11).

Lumos Learning recognizes there is no one-size-fits-all approach to build fluency in readers; however, the repeated reading of passages, where students read the same passages at least two or more times, is one of the most widely recognized strategies to improve fluency (Nichols et al., 2009). Repeated reading allows students the opportunity to read passages with familiar words several times until the passage becomes familiar and they no longer have to decode word by word. As students reread, the decoding barrier falls away allowing for an increase in reading comprehension.

The goal of the Lumos Learning workbooks is to increase student achievement and preparation for any standardized test. Using some passages multiple times in a book offers struggling readers an opportunity to do just that.

References

Hasbrouck, J., and Tindal, G. (2006). Oral reading fluency norms: A valuable assessment tool for reading teachers. Reading Teacher, 59(7), 636644. doi:10.1598/RT.59.7.3.
Nichols, W., Rupley, W., and Rasinski, T. (2009). Fluency in learning to read for meaning: going beyond repeated readings. Literacy Research & Instruction, 48(1). doi:10.1080/19388070802161906.

How Can the Lumos Study Program Prepare Students for Standardized Tests?

Since the fall of 2014, student mastery of Common Core State Standards are being assessed using standardized testing methods. At Lumos Learning, we believe that yearlong learning and adequate practice before the actual test are the keys to success on these standardized tests. We have designed the Lumos study program to help students get plenty of realistic practice before the test and to promote yearlong collaborative learning.

This is a Lumos tedBook™. It connects you to Online Workbooks and additional resources using a number of devices including Android phones, iPhones, tablets and personal computers. Each Online Workbook will have some of the same questions seen in this printed book, along with additional questions. The Lumos StepUp® Online Workbooks are designed to promote yearlong learning. The workbooks are a simple program students can securely access using a computer or device with internet access. It consists of hundreds of grade appropriate questions, aligned to the new Common Core State Standards. Students will get instant feedback and can review their answers anytime. Each student's answers and progress can be reviewed by parents and educators to reinforce the learning experience.

How to use this book effectively

The Lumos Program is a flexible learning tool. It can be adapted to suit a student's skill level and the time available to practice before standardized tests. Here are some tips to help you use this book and the online resources effectively:

Students

- The standards in each book can be practiced in the order designed, or in the order of your own choosing.
- Complete all problems in each workbook.
- Use the Online workbooks to further practice your areas of difficulty and complement classroom learning.
- Download the Lumos StepUp® app using the instructions provided in "How can I Download the App" to have anywhere access to online resources.
- Practice full length tests as you get closer to the test date.
- Complete the test in a quiet place, following the test guidelines. Practice tests provide you an opportunity to improve your test taking skills and to review topics included in the CCSS related standardized test.

Parents

- Familiarize yourself with your state's consortium and testing expectations.
- Get useful information about your school by downloading the Lumos SchoolUp™ app. Please follow directions provided in "How to download Lumos SchoolUp™ App" section of this chapter.
- Help your child use Lumos StepUp® Online Workbooks by following the instructions in "How to access the Lumos Online Workbooks" section of this chapter.
- Help your student download the Lumos StepUp® app using the instructions provided in "How can I Download the App" section of this chapter.
- Review your child's performance in the "Lumos Online Workbooks" periodically. You can do this by simply asking your child to log into the system online and selecting the subject area you wish to review.
- Review your child's work in each workbook.

Teachers

- You can use the Lumos online programs along with this book to complement and extend your classroom instruction.

- Get a Free Teacher account by using the respective states specific links and QR codes below:

PARCC States	SBAC States
LumosLearning.com/a/stepupbasic	LumosLearning.com/a/sbacbasic

This Lumos StepUp® Basic account will help you:

- Create up to 30 student accounts.
- Review the online work of your students.
- Easily access CCSS.
- Create and share information about your classroom or school events.

NOTE: There is a limit of one grade and subject per teacher for the free account.

- Download the Lumos SchoolUp™ mobile app using the instructions provided in "How can I Download the App?" section of this chapter.

How to Access the Lumos Online Workbooks

First Time Access:

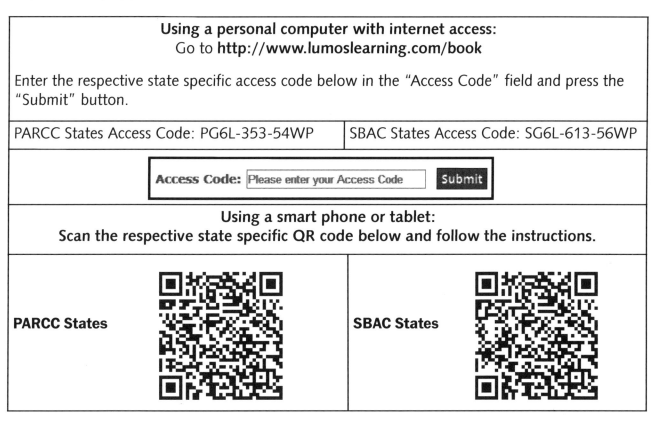

Using a personal computer with internet access:
Go to **http://www.lumoslearning.com/book**

Enter the respective state specific access code below in the "Access Code" field and press the "Submit" button.

PARCC States Access Code: PG6L-353-54WP	SBAC States Access Code: SG6L-613-56WP

Access Code: [Please enter your Access Code] **Submit**

Using a smart phone or tablet:
Scan the respective state specific QR code below and follow the instructions.

PARCC States   **SBAC States**

In the next screen, click on the "New User" button to register your user name and password.

Login
Lumos Common Core Aligned Online Workbooks - 6th Grade ELA

If you are a [New User], please register.

Login:
[ ]
Password:
[ ]
Enter

Subsequent Access:

After you establish your user id and password for subsequent access, simply login with your account information.

What if I buy more than one Lumos Study Program?

Please note that you can use all Online Workbooks with one User ID and Password. If you buy more than one book, you will access them with the same account.

Go back to the **http://www.lumoslearning.com/book** link and enter the access code provided in the second book. In the next screen simply login using your previously created account.

Lumos StepUp® Mobile App FAQ For Students

What is the Lumos StepUp® App?

It is a FREE application you can download onto your Android smart phones, tablets, iPhones, and iPads.

What are the Benefits of the StepUp® App?

This mobile application gives convenient access to Practice Tests, Common Core State Standards, Online Workbooks, and learning resources through your smart phone and tablet computers.

- Eleven Technology enhanced question types in both MATH and ELA
- Sample questions for Arithmetic drills
- Standard specific sample questions
- Instant access to the Common Core State Standards
- Jokes and cartoons to make learning fun!

Do I Need the StepUp® App to Access Online Workbooks?

No, you can access Lumos StepUp® Online Workbooks through a personal computer. The StepUp® app simply enhances your learning experience and allows you to conveniently access StepUp® Online Workbooks and additional resources through your smart phone or tablet.

How can I Download the App?

Visit **lumoslearning.com/a/stepup-app** using your smart phone or tablet and follow the instructions to download the app.

**QR Code
for Smart Phone
Or Tablet Users**

Lumos SchoolUp™ Mobile App FAQ For Parents and Teachers

What is the Lumos SchoolUp™ App?

It is a free app that teachers can use to easily access real-time student activity information as well as assign learning resources to students. Parents can also use it to easily access school-related information such as homework assigned by teachers and PTA meetings. It can be downloaded onto smart phones and tablets from popular App Stores.

What are the Benefits of the Lumos SchoolUp™ App?

It provides convenient access to
- Real-time student activity information.
- School "Stickies". A Sticky could be information about an upcoming test, homework, extra curricular activities and other school events. Parents and educators can easily create their own sticky and share with the school community.
- Discover useful educational videos and mobile apps.
- Common Core State Standards.
- Educational blogs.
- StepUp™ student activity reports.

How can I Download the App?

Visit **lumoslearning.com/a/schoolup-app** using your smartphone or tablet and follow the instructions provided to download the App. Alternatively, scan the QR Code provided below using your smartphone or tablet computer.

QR Code
for Smart Phone
Or Tablet Users

Reading: Literature

Key Ideas and Details

Analysis of Key Events and Ideas (RL.6.1)

As it poured outside, I settled down by the window to watch the rain. The green park opposite my house looked even more green and fresh than usual. Strong winds shook the branches of the tall trees. Some of the branches swayed so hard in the strong winds that I thought they would break.

Question 1

Why is the author using such clear descriptions?

(A) just to say that it was raining hard
(B) creating imagery to show the reader what that moment was like
(C) to tell us that the wind was blowing
(D) to explain what the trees look like when it rains

The Forest's Sentinel

At night, when all is still
The forest's sentinel
Glides silently across the hill
And perches in an old pine tree,
A friendly presence his!
No harm can come
From night bird on the prowl.
His cry is mellow,
Much softer than a peacock's call.
Why then this fear of owls
Calling in the night?
If men must speak,
Then owls must hoot-
They have the right.
On me it casts no spell:
Rather, it seems to cry,
"The night is good- all's well, all's well."
-- RUSKIN BOND

Question 2

From what point of view is the above poem?

Ⓐ First person point of view - from the owl's perspective
Ⓑ 3rd person point of view - from an unknown bystander or the author
Ⓒ First person point of view - from another animal's perspective
Ⓓ None of the above

Question 3

According to the above passage when does the Owl come out?

Ⓐ At night
Ⓑ At dawn
Ⓒ At dusk
Ⓓ At noon

Once upon a time four boys lived in the countryside. One boy was very clever but he did not like books. His name was Good Sense. The other boys were not very clever but they read every book in the school. When they became grown men, they decided to go out into the world to earn their livelihood.

They left home and came to a forest where they halted for the night. When they woke up in the morning, they found the bones of a lion. Three of them, who had learned their books well at school, decided to make a lion out of the bones.

Good Sense told them, "A lion is a dangerous animal. It will kill us. Don't make a lion." But the three disregarded his advice and started making a lion. Good Sense was very clever. When his friends were busy making the lion, he climbed up a tree to save himself. No sooner had the three young men created the lion and gave it life, than it pounced upon them and ate them up. Good Sense climbed down the tree and went home very sadly.

Question 4

What did they see in the forest when they woke up in the morning?

Ⓐ the bones of a lion
Ⓑ a witch that could bring an animal to life
Ⓒ Good Sense hiding in a tree
Ⓓ none of the above

Question 5

What did the four friends decide when they became grown men?

Ⓐ They decided to go out into the world and earn their livelihood.
Ⓑ They decided to play with animal bones.
Ⓒ They decided to be friends forever.
Ⓓ They decided to never leave home.

Question 6

What advice did Good Sense give his friends?

Ⓐ He told them how to create the lion.
Ⓑ He told them how to beat the lion once it was created.
Ⓒ He told them not to create the lion.
Ⓓ He told them to hide from the lion once they created it.

One evening, long after most people had gone to bed, a friend and I were making our way merrily back home through the silent and almost deserted streets. We had been to a musical show and were talking about the actor we had seen and heard in it.

"That show made him a star overnight," said my friend about one of the actors. "He was completely unknown before and now thousands of teenagers send him chocolates and love letters through the mail."

"I thought he was quite good," I said, "but not worth thousands of love letters daily. As a matter of fact, one of his songs gave me a pain."

"What was that?" my friend asked. "Sing to me." I burst into a parody of the song.

"Be quiet for heaven's sake!" My friend gave me an astonished look. "You'll give everybody a fright and wake people for miles around."

"Never mind," I said, intoxicated with the sound of my own voice. "I don't care. Why does it matter?"

And I went on singing the latest tunes at the top of my voice.

Suddenly, there came behind us the sound of heavy footsteps and before you could say "Jack Robinson" a policeman was standing in front of me, his notebook open, and a determined look on his face.

"Excuse me, sir," he said. "You have a remarkable voice, if I may say so. Who taught you to sing? I'd very much like to find someone who can give my daughter singing lessons. Would you be kind enough to tell me your name and address? Then my wife or I can drop you a line and discuss the matter."

Question 7

Why was the friend telling the man singing to be quiet?

(A) He did not like the sound of the singer's voice.
(B) He was embarrassed.
(C) He was worried that it would wake people for miles around.
(D) Because the policeman told them to be quiet.

The sky was dark and overcast. It had been raining all night long and there was no sign of it stopping. I thought that my Sunday would be ruined. As it poured outside, I settled down by the window to watch the rain. The park opposite my house looked even more green and fresh than usual. The branches of the tall trees swayed so hard in the strong wind that I thought they would break. A few children were splashing about in the mud puddles and having a wonderful time. I wished I could join them too! There were very few people out on the road and those who were hurried on their way, wrapped in raincoats and carrying umbrellas.

My mother announced that lunch was ready. It was piping hot and very welcoming in the damp weather. We spent the afternoon listening to music and to the downpour outside.

In the evening we chatted and made paper boats that we meant to sail in the stream of water outside. It was not a bad day after all!

Question 8

What detail in the above passage tells us that the writer yearned to play outside?

(A) The park opposite my house looked even more green and fresh.
(B) We spent the afternoon listening to music and to the downpour outside.
(C) I wished I could join them too!
(D) All of the above

Faster than fairies, faster than witches,
Bridges and houses, hedges and ditches,
And charging along like troops in a battle,
All through the meadows the horses and cattle,
All of the sights of the hill and the plain,
Fly as thick as driving rain,
And ever again, in the wink of an eye,
Painted stations whistle by.

Here is a child who clambers and scrambles,
All by himself and gathering brambles;
Here is a tramp who stands and gazes,
And there is the green for stinging the daisies;
Here is a cart run away in the road,
Lumping along with man and load;
And here is a mill and there is a river,
Each a glimpse and gone forever.

-- R.L.STEVENSON

Question 9

What detail in the above poem tells us that this poem is about the view from inside a train?

Ⓐ All of the sights of the hill and the plain, Fly as thick as driving rain
Ⓑ Faster than fairies, faster than witches, Bridges and houses, hedges and ditches,
Ⓒ And ever again, in the wink of an eye, Painted stations whistle by.
Ⓓ Here is a cart run away in the road

Many of the generals who had fought under Washington did not believe that the 13 colonies could cooperate to form a single country without the strong leadership of a king. They approached him, saying that they would support him as King George I of the United States. Washington was dismayed at the idea, and asked the generals to promise never to mention it again. He served two terms as President and refused a third term, retiring to his farm in Virginia. When England's King George heard that Washington had voluntarily given up the power of the presidency, he said, "If that is true, he is the greatest man in history."

Question 10

Which sentence tells you that some colonists had never known a democratic form of government?

Ⓐ   When England's King George heard that Washington had voluntarily given up the power of the presidency, he said, "If that is true, he is the greatest man in history."

Ⓑ   Washington was dismayed at the idea, and asked the generals to promise never to mention it again.

Ⓒ   He served two terms as President and refused a third term, retiring to his farm in Virginia.

Ⓓ   Many of the generals who had fought under Washington did not believe that the 13 colonies could cooperate to form a single country without the strong leadership of a king.

Conclusions Drawn from the Text (RL.6.1)

Sarah's mother told her to carry an umbrella on that Thursday morning before she left home for school, but Sarah did not want to do that. She already had her backpack and a gift for her friend to take with her. She just did not think it was necessary.

Question 1

What can you infer about Sarah?

Ⓐ She is stubborn and only wants to do things if they seem right to her.
Ⓑ She does not like her mother.
Ⓒ She doesn't like getting wet.
Ⓓ She is a very obedient child.

Question 2

What can you infer about the weather on that Thursday morning?

Ⓐ it was raining
Ⓑ it was snowing
Ⓒ it was going to rain
Ⓓ it was a warm day

The boy returned home a little late from school. He threw his coat as he walked in. He walked past his parents without greeting them. He headed straight to his room, slamming the door after him. He threw himself face down on his bed and lay there.

Question 3

How is he feeling?

Ⓐ very delighted
Ⓑ very disappointed
Ⓒ very scared
Ⓓ very excited

Katie called out to her mother. The aroma of freshly brewed coffee filled the air. The sizzling sound of frying eggs reached her ears as she glided down the stairs. Now she could smell toast and bacon too. She ran to the table and sank into her seating place just as her mother walked in from the kitchen. She was ready for _____

Question 4

Complete the sentence above.

Ⓐ Dinner
Ⓑ Lunch
● Breakfast
Ⓓ Sleeping

John wanted to buy some candy at the store. When he got there he realized he forgot his money.

Question 5

What can you infer as the action that John could take that would have the most chance of succeeding?

Ⓐ John asked the store owner if he could pay him back another day.
Ⓑ John asked the store owner if he could work for the candy.
Ⓒ John walked outside and looked on the ground to see if anyone dropped money.
● John walked back home and got the money he forgot.

Once upon a time four boys lived in the countryside. One boy was very clever but he did not like books. His name was Good Sense. The other boys were not very clever but they read every book in the school. When they became grown men, they decided to go out into the world to earn their livelihood.

They left home and came to a forest where they halted for the night. When they woke up in the morning, they found the bones of a lion. Three of them, who had learnt their books well at school, decided to make a lion out of the bones.

Good Sense told them, "A lion is a dangerous animal. It will kill us. Don't make a lion." But the three disregarded his advice and started making a lion. Good Sense was very clever. When his friends were busy making the lion, he climbed up a tree to save himself. No sooner had the three young men created the lion and gave it life, than it pounced upon them and ate them up. Good Sense climbed down the tree and went home very sadly.

Question 6

Which of the following statement(s) is true about Good Sense?

Ⓐ He was very clever
Ⓑ He did not like books
Ⓒ He did not like the other boys
● Both A and B

It is recommended that people should exercise every day, particularly those who spend many hours doing sedentary activities like playing cards, reading, or playing video games.

Question 7

We can infer that when people are doing sedentary activities, they must be _____.

Ⓐ Relaxing
Ⓑ Talking
● Sitting
Ⓓ Jumping

The sky was dark and overcast. It had been raining all night long and there was no sign of it stopping. I thought that my Sunday would be ruined. As it poured outside, I settled down by the window to watch the rain. The park opposite my house looked even more green and fresh than usual. The branches of the tall trees waved frighteningly. Some of the branches swayed so hard in the strong wind that I thought they would break. A few children were splashing about in the mud puddles and having a wonderful time. I wished I could join them too! There were very few people out on the road and those who were hurried on their way, wrapped in raincoats and carrying umbrellas.

My mother announced that lunch was ready. It was piping hot and very welcoming in the damp weather. We spent the afternoon listening to music and to the downpour outside.

In the evening we chatted and made paper boats that we meant to sail in the stream of water outside. It was not a bad day after all!

Question 8

When did the above passage occur?

Ⓐ On a very nice and sunny day.
Ⓑ On a wintry day.
Ⓒ On a hot day.
Ⓓ On a rainy day.

One evening, long after most people had gone to bed, a friend and I were making our way merrily back home through the silent and almost deserted streets. We had been to a musical show and were talking about the actor we had seen and heard in it.

"That show made him a star overnight," said my friend about one of the actors. "He was completely unknown before and now thousands of teenagers send him chocolates and love letters through the mail."

"I thought he was quite good," I said, "but not worth thousands of love letters daily. As a matter of fact, one of his songs gave me a pain."

"What was that?" my friend asked. "Sing to me." I burst into a parody of the song.

"Be quiet for heaven's sake!" My friend gave me an astonished look. "You'll give everybody a fright and wake people up for miles around."

"Never mind," I said, intoxicated with the sound of my own voice. "I don't care. How does it matter?"

And I went on singing the latest tunes at the top of my voice.

Presently there came behind us the sound of heavy footsteps and before you could say "Jack Robinson" a policeman was standing in front of me, his notebook open, and a determined look on his face.

"Excuse me, sir," he said. "You have a remarkable voice, if I may say so. Who taught you to sing? I'd very much like to find someone who can give my daughter singing lessons. Would you be kind enough to tell me your name and address? Then my wife or I can drop you a line and discuss the matter."

Question 9

Which detail in the above paragraph tells us that the author of the above passage is a male?

Ⓐ "He was completely unknown before"
Ⓑ "And I went on singing the latest tunes at the top of my voice"
Ⓒ "Excuse me, sir," he said
Ⓓ "You have a remarkable voice"

The boy and his dog were watching television when they heard a loud bang. There was a thunderstorm outside and the boy guessed that lightning must have hit something. The dog started to whimper and hid under the table.
You can guess that _____.

Question 10

Complete the sentence above.

Ⓐ The dog was scared of the television show.
Ⓑ The dog was in trouble.
Ⓒ The dog was scared of the thunderstorm.
Ⓓ The dog needed to go outside.

Development of Ideas (RL.6.2)

I always try to do what I have promised to do. If I say I will arrive at 5:15, I try to be there at 5:15. I don't lie or deliberately withhold information. I don't try to trick or confuse others. My friends trust me with their secrets, and I don't tell them to anyone else. I understand that you are looking for a trustworthy employee.

Question 1

Select the concluding sentence that most completely summarizes the argument in the passage.

Ⓐ   If you are looking for an employee who doesn't lie, then you should hire me.
Ⓑ   If you are looking for an employee who needs to be at work at 5:15, then you should hire me.
Ⓒ   If you are looking for a trustworthy person, you should hire me.
Ⓓ   I believe I would make a very good employee and would love to be considered for a position at your company.

If I am chosen to be class president, I will represent you on the Student Council. I will listen to your requests and be sure that they are heard. I will show up for meetings. I will try to make our school a better place.

Question 2

Select the concluding sentence that most completely summarizes the argument in the passage.

Ⓐ   If you vote for me, I will be a good class president.
Ⓑ   I am a good leader.
Ⓒ   I will work towards scrapping exams.
Ⓓ   The food in the cafeteria is awful.

Cats do not require as much attention as dogs. Dogs love you, and they want you to love them back. Cats are independent creatures. They don't need to be petted all the time. If you go on vacation for a few days, your dog may get lonely and refuse to eat, but your cat won't care.

Question 3

Select the concluding sentence that most completely summarizes the argument in the passage.

Ⓐ If you really want a pet, it would be a good idea to get a cat and a dog.
Ⓑ If you don't have a lot of time to care for a pet, a dog is a better choice for you than a cat.
Ⓒ Vacations are a good idea if you have a cat as a pet.
Ⓓ If you don't have a lot of time to care for a pet, a cat is a better choice for you than a dog.

Question 4

Choose the best possible supporting detail to most accurately complete the statements.

1. The beach is a perfect place to take a vacation.
2. I love to laze around on the sands.
3. _____
4. That is why I love to take a vacation at the beach.

Ⓐ I love the smell of sea water.
Ⓑ I hate the smell of sea water.
Ⓒ Starfish are so cool.
Ⓓ I like to see aircraft fly.

Question 5

Choose the best possible supporting detail to most accurately complete the statements.

1. Christmas is everybody's favorite holiday.
2. One gets to do a lot of shopping.
3. _____.
4. That is why everybody loves Christmas.

Ⓐ Christmas break is boring because you don't get to see your school friends every day.
Ⓑ The school gives a lot of homework to do over the holidays.
Ⓒ Decorating the Christmas tree is a lot of work.
Ⓓ There's a spirit of giving.

One evening, long after most people had gone to bed, a friend and I were making our way merrily back home through the silent and almost deserted streets. We had been to a musical show and were talking about the actor we had seen and heard in it.

"That show made him a star overnight," said my friend about one of the actors. "He was completely unknown before and now thousands of teenagers send him chocolates and love letters through the mail."

"I thought he was quite good," I said, "but not worth thousands of love letters daily. As a matter of fact, one of his songs gave me a pain."

"Which was that?" my friend asked. "Sing to me." I burst into a parody of the song.

"Be quiet for heaven's sake!" My friend gave me an astonished look. "You'll give everybody a fright and wake people up for miles around."

"Never mind," I said, intoxicated with the sound of my own voice. "I don't care. Why does it matter?"

And I went on singing the latest tunes at the top of my voice. Presently there came behind us the sound of heavy footsteps and before you could say "Jack Robinson" a policeman was standing in front of me, his notebook open, and a determined look on his face.

"Excuse me, sir," he said. "You have a remarkable voice, if I may say so. Who taught you to sing? I'd very much like to find someone who can give my daughter singing lessons. Would you be kind enough to tell me your name and address? Then my wife or I can drop you a line and discuss the matter."

Question 6

Choose the best title for the above passage.

Ⓐ The Singer
Ⓑ A Pleasant Surprise
Ⓒ The Musical Show
Ⓓ The Policeman

The sky was dark and overcast. It had been raining all night long and there was no sign of it stopping. I thought that my Sunday would be ruined. As it poured outside, I settled down by the window to watch the rain. The park opposite my house looked even more green and fresh than usual. The branches of the tall trees swayed so hard in the strong wind that I thought they would break. A few children were splashing about in the mud puddles and having a wonderful time. I wished I could join them too! There were very few people out on the road and those who were hurried on their way, wrapped in raincoats and carrying umbrellas.

My mother announced that lunch was ready. It was piping hot and very welcoming in the damp weather. We spent the afternoon listening to music and to the downpour outside.In the evening we chatted and made paper boats that we meant to sail in the stream of water outside. It was not a bad day after all!

Question 7

What detail in the above passage tells us that it was a cloudy day?

Ⓐ The sky was dark and overcast.
Ⓑ It had been raining all night long.
Ⓒ A few children were splashing about in the mud puddles.
Ⓓ The park opposite my house looked even more green and fresh.

The girls went to the park to play on the swings as they did each day. Their mothers always told them never to talk to strangers and always stick together. No one should walk home alone.

Question 8

What message did the girls get from their mothers?

Ⓐ Stay together and stay away from strangers.
Ⓑ Only walk home alone if there is no one else to walk with you.
Ⓒ Be friendly to anyone you meet.
Ⓓ Enjoy the park and the people.

Suzanne and her brother always helped out at the shelter. They gave out food to people who would otherwise be hungry. They also gave out blankets, clothes, and jackets. Suzanne and her brother did this twice a month. When they gave these people food, blankets, clothes, and jackets, their faces lit up and they couldn't say thank you enough times.

Question 9

Which statement indicates the primary message?

Ⓐ It is always nice and rewarding to help others.
Ⓑ Giving others blankets, clothes, and food can change their lives.
Ⓒ Giving people food will allow them to not go hungry.
Ⓓ Helping others always involves giving blankets.

Allison went to swim practice and worked very hard to try and perfect her flip turn. A flip turn is a turn where you flip underwater and turn to go back in the direction that you came from. Allison practiced 1 hour before school and 3 hours after school each day. On the weekends she practiced 5 hours a day! Allison thought she would never get the flip turn down right, but she practiced and practiced. Finally, after two weeks straight of practicing, she nailed it.

Question 10

Which statement indicates the primary message?

Ⓐ If you practice less than two weeks, you won't accomplish your goal.
Ⓑ Only practice on the weekends.
Ⓒ Keep trying and don't give up.
Ⓓ Keep trying, but give up if you get too tired.

Summary of Text (RL.6.2)

One evening, long after most people had gone to bed, a friend and I were making our way merrily back home through the silent and almost deserted streets. We had been to a musical show and were talking about the actor we had seen and heard in it.

"That show made him a star overnight," said my friend about one of the actors. "He was completely unknown before and now thousands of teenagers send him chocolates and love letters through the mail."

"I thought he was quite good," I said, "but not worth thousands of love letters daily. As a matter of fact, one of his songs gave me a pain."

"What was that?" my friend asked. "Sing to me." I burst into a parody of the song.

"Be quiet for heaven's sake!" My friend gave me an astonished look. "You'll give everybody a fright and wake people up for miles around."

"Never mind," I said, intoxicated with the sound of my own voice. "I don't care. How does it matter?"

And I went on singing the latest tunes at the top of my voice.

Presently there came behind us the sound of heavy footsteps and before you could say "Jack Robinson" a policeman was standing in front of me, his notebook open, and a determined look on his face.

"Excuse me, sir," he said. "You have a remarkable voice, if I may say so. Who taught you to sing? I'd very much like to find someone who can give my daughter singing lessons. Would you be kind enough to tell me your name and address? Then my wife or I can drop you a line and discuss the matter."

Question 1

What probably happened at the end of the story?

Ⓐ Both the friends went home and had dinner
Ⓑ The writer gave the policeman his name and address.
Ⓒ The policeman arrested both the friends
Ⓓ They went to see another musical show

Thomas is on the football team, the basketball team, and the hockey team. He even likes to run when he has free time.

Question 2

By reading this you can conclude that _____?

Ⓐ Thomas does not like soccer.
Ⓑ Thomas is an athlete and is very involved.
Ⓒ Thomas only likes sports that use a ball.
Ⓓ Thomas wishes he did not play that many sports.

Michael decided to climb a ladder to get his frisbee that landed on the roof. His father always told him to be careful when using a ladder because ladders were dangerous. Michael put on his bike helmet, asked his friend to hold the ladder, and put one hand in front of the other while climbing, never letting go of the ladder.

Question 3

What can you conclude about climbing a ladder?

Ⓐ It is a lot of fun.
Ⓑ It is easy if you know what to do.
Ⓒ You should only climb a ladder if you are over 13 years old.
Ⓓ It can be very dangerous.

On the first day of school there are many supplies that a student needs. Every student needs a notebook, pencils, pens, highlighters, and the most important, a calendar.

Question 4

What sentence below most closely agrees with these sentences?

Ⓐ All of these items help a student stay organized throughout the year.
Ⓑ These items are only helpful for students who enjoy math.
Ⓒ These items are expensive, so only buy a few of them.
Ⓓ You may not need all these items to stay organized.

It is great to have a younger sibling. Some people may think it is annoying, but those people don't realize the benefits of having a younger sibling. First, a younger sibling can do your chores for you, so you don't get in trouble. Second, they can feed the animals, so you don't have to do that. Third, they can actually be fun to play with when you are stuck at home on a snow day.

Question 5

What can you summarize from this passage?

Ⓐ It is great to have younger siblings.
Ⓑ Younger siblings are annoying.
Ⓒ You only want a sibling to be older than you.
Ⓓ Being an only child is the best.

Ryan earned money each week from doing chores around the house. His mother always told him that it was his money, but he should not spend it on useless things. Ryan decided to take $5.00 out of his piggy bank and went into the candy store. He looked at all the different types of candy and spent all of his $5.00.

Question 6

What is the most important message in this passage?

Ⓐ Ryan loves candy.
Ⓑ Ryan begged for his money.
Ⓒ Ryan had a green piggy bank.
Ⓓ Ryan shared his candy with his friends.

The little girl got to pick out new furniture and decorate her room. She really liked the white bed and dresser. She decided to paint her walls pink and get a pink carpet. She was so excited to be getting a new room!

Question 7

What can you summarize about this little girl?

Ⓐ She had always had a room to herself.
Ⓑ She was excited to redo her room the way she wanted.
Ⓒ She wanted to paint her room purple.
Ⓓ Her mother wasn't happy with her decisions.

Damon was moving to another state on the other side of the country. Along the way as his family drove, they stopped in Illinois, Idaho, and South Dakota; none of the towns they stopped in were like his hometown. When he arrived in his new hometown, he was excited to be living in a different state.

Question 8

What can you summarize about this passage?

Ⓐ Damon was moving to South Dakota.
Ⓑ Damon guessed that his new hometown would not be like his old hometown, but was excited to be moving anyway.
Ⓒ Damon did not want to stop in other states along the way.
Ⓓ Damon was moving to Illinois.

The girl stood looking out the window
No one was out there, not even an animal.
The wind blew softly and rain started to fall.
The clouds rolled in and the thunder came.
The girl felt like she was looking through the window into her own mood.

Question 9

Based on this poem, what answer best describes the girl's mood?

Ⓐ The girl liked to be alone.
Ⓑ She was scared of the rain.
Ⓒ The girl was sad and unhappy.
Ⓓ The girl was excited.

A boy embarked on a journey
Not knowing where he would end up.
He packed his things and headed out West.
It took him days and days to get to where he was going.
He was nervous and scared about what may be out there.
When the boy arrived, he wasn't sure if he was ready for what was to come.

Question 10

What was the boy doing?

Ⓐ The boy was moving and starting a new life.
Ⓑ The boy was going to become an actor.
Ⓒ The boy was going to find his long lost brother.
Ⓓ The boy was going on a vacation.

Characters Responses and Changes (RL.6.3)

One evening, long after most people had gone to bed, a friend and I were making our way merrily back home through the silent and almost deserted streets. We had been to a musical show and were talking about the actor we had seen and heard in it.

"That show made him a star overnight," said my friend about one of the actors. "He was completely unknown before and now thousands of teenagers send him chocolates and love letters through the mail."

"I thought he was quite good," I said, "but not worth thousands of love letters daily. As a matter of fact, one of his songs gave me a pain."

"Which was that?" my friend asked. "Sing to me." I burst into a parody of the song.

"Be quiet for heaven's sake!" My friend gave me an astonished look. "You'll give everybody a fright and wake people up for miles around."

"Never mind," I said, intoxicated with the sound of my own voice. "I don't care. Why does it matter?"

And I went on singing the latest tunes at the top of my voice. Presently there came behind us the sound of heavy footsteps and before you could say "Jack Robinson" a policeman was standing in front of me, his notebook open, and a determined look on his face.

"Excuse me, sir," he said. "You have a remarkable voice, if I may say so. Who taught you to sing? I'd very much like to find someone who can give my daughter singing lessons. Would you be kind enough to tell me your name and address? Then my wife or I can drop you a line and discuss the matter."

Question 1

Who are the three characters in the above passage?

Ⓐ the writer, the writer's friend, and the actor
Ⓑ the writer, the writer's friend, and the singer
Ⓒ the neighbors, the policeman, and his friend
Ⓓ the writer, the writer's friend, and the policeman

Question 2

Who were the writer and his friend referring to when they were talking and said "his songs"?

Ⓐ their neighbours
Ⓑ the policeman
Ⓒ the actor who sang in the musical show
Ⓓ the friend

The sky was dark and overcast. It had been raining all night long and there was no sign of it stopping. I thought that my Sunday would be ruined. As it poured outside, I settled down by the window to watch the rain. The park opposite my house looked even more green and fresh than usual. The branches of the tall trees swayed so hard in the strong wind that I thought they would break. A few children were splashing about in the mud puddles and having a wonderful time. I wished I could join them too! There were very few people out on the road and those who were hurried on their way, wrapped in raincoats and carrying umbrellas.

My mother announced that lunch was ready. It was piping hot and very welcoming in the damp weather. We spent the afternoon listening to music and to the downpour outside.

In the evening we chatted and made paper boats that we meant to sail in the stream of water outside. It was not a bad day after all!

Question 3

Who is the main character in the above passage?

Ⓐ The rain
Ⓑ The writer's mom
Ⓒ The writer
Ⓓ The wind

Question 4

The character in a story who dominates is a _____.

Ⓐ minor character
Ⓑ major character
Ⓒ supporting character
Ⓓ Joker

Sally woke up earlier than she expected one morning. Something wasn't right. She then realized what had awakened her. It was an unfamiliar sound. She listened closely and realized that the sound was coming from outside. Climbing out of her bed, she slipped into her robe and slippers and went to the window. Looking out, she soon spotted a small kitten under the tree that stood outside her window. She stood staring at the helpless creature. It didn't move. It soon spotted her and meowed, as if it were calling out to her.

Sally left her room and found her mother in the kitchen. She excitedly told her mom about the kitten. "I am going outside to get the poor little thing," she told her mother.

"I'll go with you," her mom replied. Together they walked into the backyard. The kitten was still there waiting for them. Sally picked it up in her arms. The little kitten felt so soft and cuddly. She had always wanted a kitten, and wondered if her mother would allow her to keep him. Mother decided to first feed the kitten. She also decided to make a few calls to see where he came from. The kitten certainly needed a home. Sally became more hopeful that she would be able to keep the kitten.

Question 5

The characters in the story are _____.

Ⓐ the kitten
Ⓑ the mother
Ⓒ Sally
Ⓓ All of the above

Question 6

The main character in a story is usually known as the _____.

Ⓐ Protagonist
Ⓑ Antagonist
Ⓒ One who saves everyone
Ⓓ The one who messes everything up

Question 7

The descriptions given by an author about the characters personality, habits, likes and dislikes are called?

Ⓐ Character style
Ⓑ Character flaws
Ⓒ Character traits
Ⓓ Character ideas

Question 8

Having to start at a new school didn't worry Jane at all; she was ready for anything.

A character trait of Jane is _____.

Ⓐ Easy-going
Ⓑ Shy
Ⓒ Scared
Ⓓ Nervous

Question 9

Realizing his son's dog was still in the burning building, the dad ran back into the building.

A character trait of the father is _____.

Ⓐ Nervous
Ⓑ Scared
Ⓒ Carefree
Ⓓ Selfless

Question 10

Ever since Greg was little, he always liked to take things apart. He took apart his sister's dolls, took apart all his trucks and cars, and even took apart his parents' telephone to see how it worked.

A character trait of Greg is_____?

Ⓐ Destructive
Ⓑ Angry
Ⓒ Curious
Ⓓ Mean

Figurative Words and Phrases (RL.6.4)

Question 1

Choose the sentence below that is closest in meaning to the figurative expression.

Edgar was dead to the world when we got home.

A Edgar was asleep when we got home.
B Edgar was not moving or breathing.
C Edgar had a head injury and was unconscious.
D Edgar was not at home.

Question 2

Choose the sentence below that is closest in meaning to the figurative expression.

You'd better go home; you're in hot water.

A You'd better go home; you're in trouble
B You'd better go home; you'll find hot water there.
C You'd better go home; you are sweating.
D You'd better go home and drink hot water.

Question 3

Choose the sentence below that is closest in meaning to the figurative expression.

He put all the papers in the circular file.

A He put the papers in the wastebasket.
B He rolled up all the papers.
C He put the papers in the round file cabinet.
D He put the papers on the circular table.

Question 4

Choose the word below that is closest in meaning to the figurative expression.

He works like a _____.

A Lion
B Dog
C Parrot
D Cat

Question 5

Choose the word below that is closest in meaning to the figurative expression.

He is as stubborn as a _____.

Ⓐ Mule
Ⓑ Cow
Ⓒ Baby
Ⓓ Ice

Question 6

Choose the sentence below that is closest in meaning to the figurative expression.

The secretary had a mountain of paper work. _____.

Ⓐ The secretary was dealing with paper art
Ⓑ The secretary had a large amount of work
Ⓒ The secretary had to run around a lot
Ⓓ The secretary had to meet a lot of people

Question 7

Choose the sentence below that is closest in meaning to the figurative expression.

His room is a train wreck. It is _____.

Ⓐ full of toy trains
Ⓑ well organized
Ⓒ a mess
Ⓓ well laid out

Question 8

Choose the sentence below that is closest in meaning to the figurative expression.

He is a star. He _____.

Ⓐ he loves soccer
Ⓑ wants to be an astronomer
Ⓒ acts in films
Ⓓ is very good at what he does

Question 9

Choose the sentence below that is closest in meaning to the figurative expression.

She is my rock. She always _____ me.

Ⓐ puts me down
Ⓑ leans on
Ⓒ criticizes
Ⓓ supports

Question 10

Choose the word below that is closest in meaning to the figurative expression.

I feel like a million bucks. I am _____.

Ⓐ Elated
Ⓑ Happy
Ⓒ Discontented
Ⓓ Both A & B

Connotative Words and Phrases (RL.6.4)

Question 1

Choose the best word to complete each sentence.

My friend is very careful about spending money. I admire that, so I call him _____.

- Ⓐ Thrifty
- Ⓑ Stingy
- Ⓒ Miserly
- Ⓓ Selfish

Question 2

Choose the best word to complete each sentence.

My friend is very careful about spending money. I don't like that trait, so I call him _____.

- Ⓐ Thrifty
- Ⓑ Stingy
- Ⓒ Rude
- Ⓓ Mean

Question 3

Choose the best word to complete each sentence.

I admire the man who jumped on the subway tracks to rescue a stranger. He was certainly _____.

- Ⓐ Foolhardy
- Ⓑ Undecided
- Ⓒ Courageous
- Ⓓ Stupid

Faster than fairies, faster than witches,
Bridges and houses, hedges and ditches,
And charging along like troops in a battle,
All through the meadows the horses and cattle,

All of the sights of the hill and the plain,
Fly as thick as driving rain,
And ever again, in the wink of an eye,
Painted stations whistle by.

Here is a child who clambers and scrambles,
All by himself and gathering brambles;
Here is a tramp who stands and gazes,
And there is the green for stinging the daisies;
Here is a cart run away in the road,
Lumping along with man and load;
And here is a mill and there is a river,
Each a glimpse and gone forever.

-- R.L.STEVENSON

Question 4

In the above poem what does the word "brambles" mean?

Ⓐ People
Ⓑ crowds of people
Ⓒ train stations
Ⓓ Prickly blue- and blackberry bushes

The girls on the playground were playing hopscotch. They all played together at recess ev-ery day. The new girl sat at the corner of the playground by herself, so one of the girls was _____ and asked her if she wanted to join them.

Question 5

Which word best completes the sentence?

Ⓐ Snotty
Ⓑ Proud
Ⓒ Friendly
Ⓓ Clever

Micky and Janie live in a quiet neighborhood and are very sweet and polite. However, the husband and wife are upset by their noisy neighbors.

Question 6

Which of the following represents what they might say to their neighbors?

Ⓐ Hey! Shut up over there!
Ⓑ Hello...would you mind keep the noise level down? We have sleeping children over here.
Ⓒ How dare you make this much noise when we have sleeping children over here!
Ⓓ If you don't get quiet in the next 5 minutes, we're calling the cops!

The first aid supplies that were brought after the hurricane were _____. Even after they came, the survivors of the hurricane kept looking for supplies.

Question 7

Which word best completes the sentence?

Ⓐ Inadequate
Ⓑ Helpful
Ⓒ Tragic
Ⓓ Important

Question 8

Skipping school can _____ your future.

What word best fits in the blank?

Ⓐ Effect
Ⓑ Help
Ⓒ Affect
Ⓓ None of the above

Question 9

The _____ candidate put his hands high in the sky and pumped his arms with a huge smile on his face.

What word best fits in the blank?

Ⓐ Unhappy
Ⓑ Bewildered
Ⓒ Victorious
Ⓓ Fun

Question 10

Jackie read the newspaper and found out that there was a twister that hit Alabama and her heart broke for the affected families. The twister wiped out hundreds of houses. This was such a _____ event.

What word best fits in the blank?

Ⓐ Exciting
Ⓑ Tragic
Ⓒ Unimportant
Ⓓ Victorious

Meaning of Words and Phrases (RL.6.4)

"That show made him a star overnight", said my friend about one of the actors. "He was completely unknown before. And now thousands of teenagers send him chocolates and love letters in the mail."

Question 1

What does the above paragraph mean?

- Ⓐ that the actor had poor acting skills
- Ⓑ that the actor had come to fame recently
- Ⓒ that nobody likes him now
- Ⓓ none of the above

The forest's sentinel
Glides silently across the hill
And perches in an old pine tree,
A friendly presence his!
No harm can come
From night bird on the prowl.
His cry is mellow,

Much softer than a peacock's call.
Why then this fear of owls
Calling in the night?
If men must speak,
Then owls must hoot-
They have the right.
On me it casts no spell:
Rather, it seems to cry,
"The night is good- all's well, all's well."

-- RUSKIN BOND

Question 2

What is the poet talking about in the first stanza?

Ⓐ how the owl comes out into the night
Ⓑ how the owl catches its prey
Ⓒ how the owl is looking into the dark night
Ⓓ how the owl walks

Question 3

What is the poet saying about the owl?

Ⓐ He is comparing the owl to a sentinel
Ⓑ He is describing the flight of the owl
Ⓒ He is saying that the owl is friendly and harmless
Ⓓ All of the above

The sky was dark and overcast. It had been raining all night long and there was no sign of it stopping. I thought that my Sunday would be ruined. As it poured outside, I settled down by the window to watch the rain. The park opposite my house looked even more green and fresh than usual. The branches of the tall trees swayed so hard in the strong wind that I thought they would break. A few children were splashing about in the mud puddles and having a wonderful time. I wished I could join them too! There were very few people out on the road and those who were hurried on their way, wrapped in raincoats and carrying umbrellas.

My mother announced that lunch was ready. It was piping hot and very welcoming in the damp weather. We spent the afternoon listening to music and to the downpour outside.

In the evening we chatted and made paper boats that we meant to sail in the stream of water outside. It was not a bad day after all.

Question 4

How does the writer end the passage?

Ⓐ With a satisfied tone
Ⓑ With a sad tone
Ⓒ With a annoyed tone
Ⓓ With an excited tone

Androcles was a slave who escaped from his master and fled to the forest. As he was wandering there, he came upon a lion lying down moaning and groaning. Seeing the lion in pain, he removed a huge thorn from the beast's paw. After this incident, they lived together as great friends in the forest. Androcles was eventually arrested and condemned to death in the arena. He would be thrown to a lion which was captured and not given food for several days. The Emperor and his courtiers came to see the spectacle. Androcles was lead to the middle of the arena and so was the hungry lion. The lion roared and rushed towards its victim. But, as soon as he came near Androcles, he recognized him and licked his hands like a friendly dog. Everyone was surprised. The emperor heard the whole story and pardoned Androcles and freed the lion to his native forest.

Question 5

This story brings out the meaning of _____.

Ⓐ Friendship
Ⓑ Slavery
Ⓒ Escape
Ⓓ Hunger

Last week, I fell off my bike and hurt myself badly. I bruised my elbow and sprained my wrist. My injuries would have been worse if I hadn't been wearing my bicycle helmet. My doctor asked me to tell this to all my friends so that they would wear helmets too. I told my teacher and she asked me to make a public announcement during the school assembly. I had to talk about the accident and how the helmet protected me.

Question 6

Why was I asked to tell everyone about my accident and mention wearing the helmet?

Ⓐ so that everyone understands the benefit of wearing a helmet
Ⓑ because it made an interesting story
Ⓒ so that everyone comes to know what a hero I am
Ⓓ so that helmets can be sold

Life and death were ideal as they crept into the dark world.

Question 7

What is the mood of this sentence?

Ⓐ Ominous
Ⓑ Tragic
Ⓒ Dramatic
Ⓓ Silly

The man was feeble-minded and did not realize when others made fun of him by laughing at him and talking behind his back.

Question 8

What is the tone of this sentence?

Ⓐ Unconcerned
Ⓑ Upsetting
Ⓒ Angry
Ⓓ Rude

My brother comes in my room and hides my dolls,
but my brother plays hide and seek with me.
My brother tells me I'm annoying and should leave his room,
but my brother stands up for me on the playground when someone is mean to me.
My brother plays with his friends and tells me I'm too young to join them,
but my brother plays with me in the snow when we have a snow day.

Question 9

What is the hidden meaning in the poem?

Ⓐ The brother easily gets frustrated with his sibling.
Ⓑ The brother doesn't want to play with his sibling.
Ⓒ The brother really loves his sibling.
Ⓓ The brother likes to play with dolls.

Without you here, I can move forward
Thinking of the past only makes it worse,
Forgetting is the only way to continue on

Question 10

Ⓐ The narrator is angry at someone
Ⓑ The narrator is moving away
Ⓒ The narrator wants to think of all the memories
Ⓓ The narrator wants to move forward; it is too sad to look back

Develop Setting (RL.6.5)

The sky was dark and overcast. It had been raining all night long and there was no sign of it stopping. I thought that my Sunday would be ruined. As it poured outside, I settled down by the window to watch the rain. The park opposite my house looked even more green and fresh than usual. The branches of the tall trees swayed so hard in the strong wind that I thought they would break. A few children were splashing about in the mud puddles and having a wonderful time. I wished I could join them too! There were very few people out on the road and those who were hurried on their way, wrapped in raincoats and carrying umbrellas.

My mother announced that lunch was ready. It was piping hot and very welcoming in the damp weather. We spent the afternoon listening to music and to the downpour outside.

In the evening we chatted and made paper boats that we meant to sail in the stream of water outside. It was not a bad day after all!

Question 1

What is the setting of the above story

Ⓐ The home of the writer
Ⓑ The park
Ⓒ The writer's village
Ⓓ The writer's office

One evening, long after most people had gone to bed, a friend and I were making our way merrily back home through the silent and almost deserted streets. We had been to a musical show and were talking about the actor we had seen and heard in it.

"That show made him a star overnight," said my friend about one of the actors. "He was completely unknown before and now thousands of teenagers send him chocolates and love letters through the mail."

"I thought he was quite good," I said, "but not worth thousands of love letters daily. As a matter of fact, one of his songs gave me a pain."

"Which was that?" my friend asked. "Sing to me." I burst into a parody of the song.

"Be quiet for heaven's sake!" My friend gave me an astonished look. "You'll give everybody a fright and wake people up for miles around."

"Never mind," I said, intoxicated with the sound of my own voice. "I don't care.

How does it matter?"

And I went on singing the latest tunes at the top of my voice. Presently there came behind us the sound of heavy footsteps and before you could say "Jack Robinson" a policeman was standing in front of me, his notebook open, and a determined look on his face.

"Excuse me, sir," he said. "You have a remarkable voice, if I may say so. Who taught you to sing? I'd very much like to find someone who can give my daughter singing lessons. Would you be kind enough to tell me your name and address? Then my wife or I can drop you a line and discuss the matter."

Question 2

What detail in the above story tells us that it took place late in the night?

Ⓐ We had been to a musical show
Ⓑ "Be quiet for heaven's sake."
Ⓒ One evening, long after most people had gone to bed
Ⓓ And I went on singing the latest tunes at the top of my voice

Sally woke up earlier than she expected one morning. Something wasn't right. She then realized what had awakened her. It was an unfamiliar sound. She listened closely and realized that the sound was coming from outside. Climbing out of her bed, she slipped into her robe and slippers and went to the window. Looking out, she soon spotted a small kitten under the tree that stood outside her window. She stood staring at the helpless creature. It didn't move. It soon spotted her and meowed, as if it were calling out to her.

Sally left her room and found her mother in the kitchen having her morning cup of coffee. She excitedly told her mom about the kitten. "I am going outside to get the poor little thing," she told her mother.

"I'll go with you," her mom replied. Together they walked into the backyard. The kitten was still there waiting for them. Sally picked it up in her arms. The little kitten felt so soft and cuddly in her arms. She had always wanted a kitten, and wondered if her mother would allow her to keep him. Mother decided to first feed the kitten. She also decided to make a few calls to see where he came from. The kitten certainly needed a home. Sally became more hopeful that she would be able to keep the kitten.

Question 3

What sentence(s) point(s) out the time of the story?

Ⓐ Sally went out of her room and found her mother in the kitchen having her morning cup of coffee

Ⓑ Sally went out of her room and found her mother in the kitchen.

Ⓒ Sally woke up earlier than she expected one morning.

Ⓓ Both A and C

Question 4

From the story, we come to know that Sally lived _____.

Ⓐ in a multi-storied building

Ⓑ in a dowtown, urban area

Ⓒ in a motel

Ⓓ in a single family house with a backyard

The forest's sentinel
Glides silently across the hill
And perches in an old pine tree,
A friendly presence his!
No harm can come
From night bird on the prowl.
His cry is mellow,
Much softer than a peacock's call.

Why then this fear of owls
Calling in the night?
If men must speak,
Then owls must hoot-
They have the right.
On me it casts no spell:
Rather, it seems to cry,
"The night is good- all's well, all's well."

-- RUSKIN BOND

Question 5

The setting of this poem is in a _____.

Ⓐ Sports stadium
Ⓑ Forest
Ⓒ House
Ⓓ Palace

Question 6

What is the setting of a story?

Ⓐ Who and where the story takes place
Ⓑ When and where the story takes place
Ⓒ When and why the story takes place
Ⓓ How and where the story takes place

Question 7

Ralphie lived in the oldest and largest house on the block. Ralphie's friends were scared to visit him because of how worn down his house looked. The outside of the house was gray with cracks in the stucco and lots of spider webs hanging off it.

What is the setting of the story?

Ⓐ Inside Ralphie's house
Ⓑ Inside Ralphie's friends' houses
Ⓒ Outside Ralphie's house
Ⓓ None of the above

Question 8

The thieves intended to rob the bank around dinner time. They figured most people would be home eating with their families, so it would be easy for them to get in and out of the big green and gold bank.

What is the setting of the story?

Ⓐ The bank on Green Street
Ⓑ The bank on Green Street at 7pm
Ⓒ The green and gold bank at dinner time
Ⓓ The green and gold bank in the morning

Janice had her last final exam of the year; she was very excited and wanted to celebrate. After this final, she would no longer be a high school student.

Question 9

In what month was it most likely this last exam occurred?

Ⓐ In April
Ⓑ In June
Ⓒ In September
Ⓓ In December

Noah was excited that he got to share his birthday with his aunt. They were both born on the same day, just nineteen years apart. Their birthday was on April 13th.

Question 10

In what season is Noah's birthday?

Ⓐ In the spring
Ⓑ In the summer
Ⓒ In the winter
Ⓓ In the fall

Author's Purpose in a Text (RL.6.6)

In the original version of the story "The Three Little Pigs," the wolf chases the pigs and says he will huff and puff and blow their houses down.

The following paragraph is a different interpretation.

I've always been misunderstood. I'm allergic to hay. I can't help it that when I'm near hay, I huff and I puff and I sometimes blow things down. Also, I'm a vegetarian so I would never eat a pig! No one has any reason to be afraid of me, but sometimes they are. What happened to those poor little pigs is sad, but it was their own fault.

Question 1

Who is talking in this passage? _____

Ⓐ The pigs in the story "The Three Little Pigs."
Ⓑ The wolf in the story "The Three Little Pigs."
Ⓒ A 3rd person narrator
Ⓓ The bird watching everything

Question 2

How is the narrator's point of view different from the traditional one?

Ⓐ He claims that he had no intention of blowing down the pigs' houses or of eating them, but that his allergies were at fault
Ⓑ He claims that he had no intention of blowing down the pigs' house, but wanted to eat them up.
Ⓒ He claims that he had no intention of blowing down the pigs' houses or of eating them, but he just wanted to scare them.
Ⓓ He claims that another wolf blew the pigs' houses down and blamed it on him.

Question 3

Why does the narrator claim to have been misunderstood?

Ⓐ Because everyone has regarded him as a bully who wants to occupy weaker animals' houses
Ⓑ Because everyone has regarded him as a pig-killing villain when he had no such intention.
Ⓒ Because everyone has regarded him sick and allergy-ridden.
Ⓓ Because he is evil.

I was shaking like a leaf. My palms were sweaty and I was so nervous about my presentation.

Question 4

What point of view is this from?

Ⓐ Third person omniscient
Ⓑ Second person
Ⓒ First person
Ⓓ Third person

Heather loved her new dog. She played with it every day and took it for walks. The dog became Heather's best friend, and they did everything together.

Question 5

What point of view is this told in?

Ⓐ First person
Ⓑ Second person
Ⓒ Third person
Ⓓ None of the above

In the original version of "Little Red Riding Hood," Red is delivering food to her sick grandmother when she stumbles upon a wolf in the house.

The following is a different interpretation of "Little Red Riding Hood,"

I'd been after that wolf for a long time, but when I went into the woods that day to deliver a basket to my grandmother, I promised my mother that I wouldn't leave the path to go wolf-hunting, even if I got a clear shot. I even spoke politely to him and did exactly as my mother asked. But when I got to grandma's house, I found that he had eaten her! I was determined to get revenge. Thank goodness the woodcutter came along and did my job for me. I don't need to get into any trouble with my mother, but it really burns me up when people think I couldn't have handled the wolf by myself!

Question 6

Who is talking in this passage?

Ⓐ Red Riding Hood in the story "Little Red Riding Hood"
Ⓑ The wolf in the story "Little Red Riding Hood"
Ⓒ The mother in the story "Little Red Riding Hood"
Ⓓ A narrator

Question 7

How is the narrator's point of view different from the traditional one?

Ⓐ She is traditionally thought of as a brave girl who wanted to fight the wily wolf.
Ⓑ The narrator's point of view is not different from the traditional one.
Ⓒ She is traditionally thought of as an innocent child, in danger from the wily wolf.
Ⓓ She is thought of as a mean girl who hates wolfs.

Question 8

Why does the narrator claim to have been misunderstood?

Ⓐ she wanted people to think that she is a brave girl
Ⓑ people think she couldn't have defeated the wolf
Ⓒ people think that she does not follow her mother's instructions
Ⓓ both A and B

The forest's sentinel
Glides silently across the hill
And perches in an old pine tree,
A friendly presence his!
No harm can come
From night bird on the prowl.
His cry is mellow,
Much softer than a peacock's call.

Why then this fear of owls
Calling in the night?
If men must speak,
Then owls must hoot-
They have the right.
On me it casts no spell:
Rather, it seems to cry,
"The night is good- all's well, all's well."

-- RUSKIN BOND

Question 9

In the above poem the author says 'If men must speak, Then owls must hoot-They have the right.' What does he mean by this?

Ⓐ That people should hoot like owls.
Ⓑ That owls should talk like people.
Ⓒ That owls hoot for the same reasons people speak. This is the way owls com municate.
Ⓓ That owls do not have the right to talk.

Question 10

Which of the following are usually written in the second person point of view?

Ⓐ Instructions
Ⓑ Self-help books
Ⓒ Directions
Ⓓ All of the above

Name: _____   Date: _____

Integration of Knowledge and Ideas

Compare Authors Writing to Another (RL.6.9)

If your actions inspire others to dream more, learn more, do more and become more, you are a leader. - John Quincy Adams

The key to successful leadership today is influence, not authority.- Kenneth Blanchard

Question 1

A look at both the above statements tells us that they are talking about _____.

- Ⓐ friendship
- Ⓑ leadership
- Ⓒ actions
- Ⓓ dreams

Read the following passage and answer the question that follows.

The square is probably the best known of the quadrilaterals. It is defined as having all sides equal. All its interior angles are right angles (90°). From this it follows that the opposite sides are also parallel. A square is simply a specific case of a regular polygon, in this case with 4 sides. All the facts and properties described for regular polygons apply to a square.

The rectangle, like the square, is one of the most commonly known quadrilaterals. It is defined as having all four interior angles 90° (right angles). The opposite sides of a rectangle are parallel and congruent.

Question 2

A similarity between a square and rectangle is that _____.

- Ⓐ all the sides are equal in both the figures
- Ⓑ only opposite sides are equal in both the figures
- Ⓒ all the interior angles are right angles
- Ⓓ none of the angles are right angles

Question 3

A difference between a square and rectangle is that _____.

Ⓐ all sides are equal in a square, whereas only opposite sides are equal in a rectangle
Ⓑ all the interior angles are right angles
Ⓒ only opposite sides are equal in both the figures
Ⓓ both are quadrilaterals

Read the statements carefully and answer the question that follow.

1. Teachers who inspire know that teaching is like cultivating a garden, and those who would have nothing to do with thorns must never attempt to gather flowers.
~Author Unknown

2. Teachers who inspire realize that there will always be rocks in the road ahead of us. They will be stumbling blocks or stepping stones; it all depends on how we use them.
~Author Unknown

Question 4

While the first author says that teaching is like cultivating a garden, the second author says that _____.

Ⓐ those teachers who would have nothing to do with thorns must never attempt to gather flowers
Ⓑ inspiring teachers realize that there will be rocks in the road ahead
Ⓒ inspiring teachers realize that there will only be stepping stones in the road
Ⓓ inspiring teachers realize that there will be only flowers and no thorns

Question 5

Both the quotations are about _____.

Ⓐ stumbling blocks
Ⓑ rocks and stepping stones
Ⓒ gardens, flowers and thorns
Ⓓ teachers who inspire

Question 6

Hurricanes are similar to blizzards because _____.

Ⓐ They both are rain storms.
Ⓑ They both cause heavy destruction.
Ⓒ They both are man-made storms.
Ⓓ They both involve snow.

Question 7

Love is _____ to a roller coaster because there are many twists in turns in both.

Ⓐ different
Ⓑ unequal
Ⓒ similar
Ⓓ All of the above

Question 8

When you wash dishes you want to make sure you use soap to scrub the dirt off and make sure you rinse them clean after.

Which of the tasks below are similar to washing dishes?

Ⓐ Cleaning your house
Ⓑ Washing the laundry
Ⓒ Folding your clothes
Ⓓ Cooking dinner

Question 9

Words that are used to compare things are _____.

Ⓐ Like
Ⓑ Same as
Ⓒ Both A and B
Ⓓ In Contrast

Question 10

A word that is used to contrast two things is _____.

Ⓐ Too
Ⓑ However
Ⓒ More
Ⓓ And

End of Reading: Literature

Answer Key and Detailed Explanations

Reading: Literature

Analysis of Key Events and Ideas (RL.6.1)

Question No.	Answer	Detailed Explanations
1	B	The author is giving information and is not telling a specific story, trying to convince someone of something, or trying to entertain. Although there is some personality in the writing and it is very interesting, you must look at the fact that almost all of the sentences in the paragraph give information; therefore, it is informative.
2	B	Although the author is talking about the night owl, the point of view is actually that of the author.
3	A	The poem mentions that it's a night bird and, at the end, again mentions night. The answer is A.
4	A	Answer A is correct. Upon reading the passage, you will see in the second paragraph that it directly says that they found the bones of a lion.
5	A	If you chose A, you read the passage correctly. The last sentence in the first paragraph gives the correct answer.
6	C	If you chose answer C, you got it right. Good Sense told the other men NOT to create the lion.
7	C	Answer C is the correct answer because it's a direct quote in the story that the friend was afraid the singing would disturb others. The policeman was not behind them yet, or at least had not been noticed. There was no mention of the friend being embarrassed.
8	C	The only answer choice that shows a desire to play outside is C.
9	C	Answer choice C is correct. The fact that it goes by stations tells you that you're on a train.
10	D	If you selected D, you picked the right answer. The fact that the generals did not think it was possible to form a central government without a king shows that they had never known a democratic system.

Conclusions Drawn from the Text (RL.6.1)

Question No.	Answer	Detailed Explanations
1	A	The correct answer is A. Sarah's mother told her that it was going to rain, but Sarah chose to ignore her mother's advice. None of the other answers are true. There is no evidence that she doesn't love her mother, and if she didn't like getting wet then she would have definitely have listened to her mother. She did not obey her mother, so answer choice D is not correct.
2	C	The correct answer is C. Sarah would not have argued about whether or not to take an umbrella if it were raining. She would not need an umbrella if it were snowing or if it were warm.
3	B	The correct answer is B. We can tell that it is a negative emotion that the boy is feeling - so that eliminates A and D. If he were scared, he would likely want to be WITH people, not away from them.
4	C	The correct answer is C. All of the foods mentioned were breakfast foods, so you can assume that breakfast is being cooked. Also, coffee is usually brewed first thing in the morning.
5	D	In this day and age, it is not likely that the store owner would let him pay him later or work off the candy. John would have to go home and get the money and walk back to the store.
6	D	D is the correct answer. The story specifically says that he did not like books and that he was very clever. Nothing was said in the story that he did not like the other boys.
7	C	The correct answer is C. If the article is saying that these people need to be active, then we can assume that they normally do a lot of sitting.
8	D	The answer is D. The passage specifically says that it was raining and there was no sign of it stopping. The passage does not mention wintry weather or sunny day.
9	C	The answer is C. The fact that the officers called him sir is the only detail that shows that it is a male.
10	C	The correct answer is C. The dog hid under the table AFTER the loud noise, so we can assume that the dog was scared by the loud noises associated with the thunderstorm.

Development of Ideas (RL.6.2)

Question No.	Answer	Detailed Explanations
1	D	The correct answer is D because it is a good ending sentence and sums up the point of the paragraph. A and B are too specific, and C is repetitive.
2	A	The only answer that is a concluding sentence is answer choice A. It mentions class president, which is the point of the article. The other three answers are specific details and do not sum up the passage.
3	D	Answer choice D is correct. It correctly summarizes the point of the article. The other three answers do not make sense if you read the passage carefully.
4	A	The correct answer is A. Loving the smell of sea water supports loving the beach as far as a vacation trip. Although there are starfish in the ocean and sometimes aircraft fly by, neither of those details support the main idea of the paragraph. The author would not like vacationing at the beach if he/she hated the smell of sea water, so B is not correct.
5	D	Answer choice D is correct. All of the statements about Christmas are positive, so this detail will be positive too. All of the other answer choices are negative.
6	B	While all of the titles make sense, the best title would be B, "A Pleasant Surprise." The character in the story was very pleasantly surprised that he was not in trouble with the policeman.
7	A	The correct answer is A. Although all of the answers are true statements, the only one that gives the detail of the sky being cloudy is saying it is "dark and overcast."
8	A	The correct answer is A. The mothers specifically told the girls to stay together and stay away from strangers. Answer choices B and C are opposite of what the mothers told their daughters.
9	A	Answer A is the correct choice. The primary message of the passage is that it is rewarding to help others. Although giving people food helps them not to go hungry, it is only one detail of the passage. There is no evidence to show receiving the items changes people's lives, and helping others does not always mean giving blankets.
10	C	The correct answer is C. Allison worked very hard and did not give up, and she eventually accomplished her goal. A is not correct because it will take people different amounts of time to accomplish what they set out to do. The key is to never give up. D is the opposite of what the passage is saying, and B is never mentioned.

Summary of Text (RL.6.2)

Question No.	Answer	Detailed Explanations
1	B	Answer choice B is correct because the story specifically says that the policeman asked the writer for his name and address. You assume that the man gave it to him.
2	B	The correct answer is B. Based on the fact that Thomas plays so many sports and runs; you can assume that he is an athlete. The article does not say anything about which sports Thomas does and doesn't like. It also does not mention anything about Thomas not wanting to play that many sports.
3	D	Because he is being so careful, you know that ladders can be dangerous. The correct answer is D. Age is never mentioned, neither is ladders being easy or fun.
4	A	The correct answer is A. The paragraph mentions nothing about students who enjoy math and it doesn't mention how many to buy. It also does not say anything about not needing all of the items.
5	A	The passage is positive about younger siblings, so the answer choice will be positive. It is obvious that the author of the passage thinks that having younger siblings is great.
6	A	The correct answer is A. Because he spent all of the 5 dollars at the candy store, you can assume that he loves candy and did not think spending the money would be useless. That is the only answer that could be right. It never mentions what color his piggy bank is or sharing his candy.
7	B	The correct answer is B. It does not mention whether or not she has had her own room before or not. Her mother is not even mentioned and it said she was decorating her room pink, not purple.
8	B	The correct answer is B. The passage does not mention what state he is moving to, and it also does not mention that he didn't want to stop in other states along the way.
9	C	Answer choice C is correct because the poem has a sad mood. The girl is feeling sad and unhappy. It does not mention that she is afraid and we know that she is not excited. Even though she went to her room, it does not mention that she wanted to be alone.
10	A	Based on the passage, the boy was moving to start a new life. They did not say that he was going on vacation, trying to make it as an actor, or looking for his brother. That's why we can assume that he is starting a new life.

Characters Responses and Changes (RL.6.3)

Question No.	Answer	Detailed Explanations
1	D	Answer choice D is correct. There are only three characters in the story; the writer, the writer's friend, and the policeman. Although the actor is mentioned, he is not an actual character.
2	C	The correct answer is C. They were talking about the man in the musical show they had just seen.
3	C	The correct answer is C. The writer is writing in 1st person, and she is the main character in her story.
4	B	The correct answer is B. A major character will be a major part of the story. They will be in more of the story than minor characters.
5	D	The answer is D, all of the above. If you missed this question, go back and re-read the story. Each of these characters contributed action to the story.
6	A	The correct answer is A. The protagonist is often the good guy in a story. He/she is the main character of the story.
7	C	Character traits are the descriptions that authors give their characters. The answer is C.
8	A	Jane was very positive about starting a new school, so we are looking for a positive answer. They are all negative emotions except easy-going.
9	D	The answer choice is D. Risking his own life to save a dog's life shows the man thinks of others more than himself.
10	C	Greg was trying to see how things worked, not being mean to people. The answer choice is C. He was curious.

Figurative Words and Phrases (RL.6.4)

Question No.	Answer	Detailed Explanations
1	A	The answer is A. "dead to the world" means that he was asleep. He would not stay at home if he was not breathing or unconscious; he would be removed immediately and his family would be upset.
2	A	Being in hot water means being in trouble, so answer choice A is correct.
3	A	The correct answer is A. There is no such thing as a circular file, so the only possibility is the trashcan. To say that means to throw something away.
4	B	Working like a dog means working really hard, so answer choice B is correct. This is a common saying.
5	A	Mules are known to be stubborn, so answer choice A is correct.
6	B	A mountain of work is a lot of work. Answer choice B is correct.
7	C	A train wreck causes a big mess on the tracks. Answer choice C is correct.
8	D	Being a star doesn't mean you have to be famous. When you are really good at something, you are said to be "a star". Answer choice D is correct.
9	D	Being a rock means that you are there for someone to lean on. Answer choice D is correct.
10	D	When someone says they feel like a million bucks, it means they feel great. The correct answer is D. Elated means the same thing as happy. Discontented means the opposite.

Connotative Words and Phrases (RL.6.4)

Question No.	Answer	Detailed Explanations
1	A	Thrifty means that you don't want to spend money unless you have to and you want to save as much as possible. Answer choice A is correct.
2	B	Because the author of this sentence admitted that he/she didn't like the trait, we know there is a negative spin on the part of the author. That's why the correct answer is B.
3	C	'Courageous' is the word with the positive connotation.
4	D	Brambles are prickly bushes or shrubs. It specifically says that he was "all by himself" so we know other people weren't around.
5	C	It was very nice for the girl to ask the new student to join in. C is the answer.
6	B	Because they are characterized as being "sweet and polite" we would assume their actions would be in line with that. Answer choices A and D are very rude and hateful. Answer choice B is more of the way a sweet and polite couple would react.
7	A	The fact that they had to keep looking for supplies tells us that there were not enough supplies. The correct answer is A.
8	C	Affect is the correct word for the verb in this sentence.
9	C	The positive connotation of the words in the sentence show us that the candidate won. That is why C is the correct answer
10	B	The answer is B. Tragic is the only negative word that works in this sentence.

Meaning of Words and Phrases (RL.6.4)

Question No.	Answer	Detailed Explanations
1	B	Answer choice B is correct. Based on the sentences, it is clear that the person being discussed has come to fame recently.
2	A	The first part of the poem is how the owl comes out of the tree into the forest at night. The correct answer is A.
3	D	The poet said all of the above things in the opening lines of the poem.
4	A	The author did not seem excited, but was definitely not negative (annoyed or sad.) The correct answer is A.
5	A	Because the man had helped the lion, the man's life was spared. Even though it is a human and an animal, it is a story of friendship. The correct answer is A.
6	A	The correct answer is A. The teacher asked the student to share the story so that maybe more kids would wear helmets.
7	A	Ominous is kind of creepy and spooky. That is definitely the mood here. The answer is A.
8	B	When you hear that statement, it makes you feel badly for that man. The answer choice that is correct is B.
9	C	Answer choice C is correct. Even though the brother isn't always nice to his sister, his actions show her that he loves her.
10	D	Answer choice D is correct based on the poem. The author talks about moving forward and forgetting.

Develop Setting (RL.6.5)

Question No.	Answer	Detailed Explanations
1	A	Based on the details in the passage, it is obvious that the writer is a child still living at home. They discuss doing things that would take place in a home. For those reasons, the correct answer is A.
2	C	The story specifically says that it took place long after people had gone to bed, so answer choice C is correct.
3	D	The correct answer is D. The story specifically says it is morning and she found her mother in the kitchen drinking coffee.
4	D	The correct answer is D. It couldn't be a motel because her mother was in the kitchen sipping coffee. The backyard indicates they are not in an urban area. The most logical answer is that they live in just a regular single family home.
5	B	The answer is B, a forest. The poem never mentions a sports stadium, a house or a palace, but it mentions the forest in the opening line.
6	B	The answer is B. The setting of a story is when and where a story takes place
7	C	The answer is C. The only place mentioned is the outside of Ralphie's house, so that is the only option.
8	C	The correct answer is C. The story specifically says that the robbery was going to take place during dinner time and it was going to be at the green and gold bank
9	B	Because it's her last final exam of high school, you know that the setting of the story is in June.
10	A	The correct answer is A. The month of April is definitely in the spring.

Author's Purpose in a Text (RL.6.6)

Question No.	Answer	Detailed Explanations
1	B	Based on what he says, you can tell that these words are from the wolf's perspective. Answer choice B is correct.
2	A	In the above passage the wolf claims that allergies were to blame and he didn't want to hurt the pigs. That is very different from the traditional story.
3	B	He is trying to act innocent by saying he never meant to hurt the pigs.
4	C	Because "I" is used, we know that it is written from first person point of view.
5	C	The story does not use I or you; therefore, it is written in third person.
6	A	This passage was definitely from Little Red Riding Hood's perspective. The mother is never mentioned, but the wolf is. Therefore, it can't be from his perspective.
7	C	Answer choice C is correct. She is very sweet and innocent in the original story. She believes things that most of us wouldn't.
8	D	She wanted people to think she could have handled herself just fine against the wolf and that she wasn't scared at all.
9	C	Answer choice C is correct. The author clearly says that owls have the right to hoot if men have the right to speak.
10	D	Anytime someone is giving instructions or telling you what to do, it will be written in second person. D is the correct answer.

Compare Author's Writing to Another (RL.6.9)

Question No.	Answer	Detailed Explanations
1	B	Both quotes mention leadership, so the correct answer is B. Only one quote mentions dreams and actions. Friendship is not mentioned.
2	C	Based on the passage, we know that in both figures all of the angles are 90 degree angles (right angles). The correct answer is C.
3	A	Based on the passage, all sides are equal in a square; however, in a rectangle only sides opposite of each other are equal when you measure them. The correct answer is A.
4	B	Answer choice B is correct. Upon careful reading of the passage, you will see that the author specifically says that there will be rocks in the road ahead. The author does not say the rocks will always be stepping stones; some will be stumbling.
5	D	Both passages use metaphors to describe inspirational teachers, with the rocks and thorns being symbols for obstacles in their way. The correct answer is D.
6	B	The only answer statement that is true is B. A hurricane involves rain and a snowstorm involves snow but both storms can cause heavy destruction.
7	C	Similar is the same as "like." That is why the answer is C.
8	B	Answer choice B is the most similar because you use soap and water and have to rinse and dry them.
9	C	Like and Same as are both words we use to compare things. Contrast is a word we use to tell how things are different. The answer is C.
10	B	"However" is the only word that is a word you could use to contrast something. It is similar to the word "but."

Reading Informational Text
Key Ideas and Details

Cite Textual Evidence (RI.6.1) to support analysis of what the text says explicitly as well as inferences drawn from the text.

Everywhere around us there are millions of tiny living things called germs. They are so tiny that they can be seen only under the most powerful microscope. Some of these germs are no wider than twenty-five thousandths of an inch!

Louis Pasteur, the great French scientist, was the first to prove that germs exist. The germs in the air can be counted. The number of germs around us, especially in crowded rooms, is tremendous. Certain scientists counted 42,000 germs in approximately one cubic meter of air in a picture gallery when it was empty. But when the gallery was crowded with people, they found nearly 5,000,000 germs in the same place. In the open air germs are less abundant. There are fewer germs in country air than in town air. We see at once how important it is, therefore, to live as much as possible in the open air, and for the rooms we live in to always be well ventilated by fresh air.

Question 1

According the passage, where will you find more germs?

Ⓐ In crowded spaces
Ⓑ In the country
Ⓒ In hospitals
Ⓓ In empty rooms

Question 2

Which of the following statements can be concluded after reading the passage?

Ⓐ Louis Pasteur liked counting germs.
Ⓑ Germs are too small to be seen.
Ⓒ People have germs.
Ⓓ Fresher air has fewer germs.

George Washington was the first and most popular U.S. President. He was the only one elected by a unanimous vote. It is often said of him that he was "first in war, first in peace, and first in the hearts of his countrymen." Washington led comparatively untrained and ill-equipped American soldiers to victory over the well-trained British in the Revolutionary War. As soon as the Constitution was ratified, he was chosen to be president.

Many of the generals who had fought under Washington did not believe that the 13 colonies could cooperate to form a single country without the strong leadership of a king. They approached him, saying that they would support him as King George I of the United States. Washington was dismayed at the idea, and asked the generals to promise never to mention it again. He served two terms as President and refused a third term, retiring to his farm in Virginia. When England's King George heard that Washington had voluntarily given up the power of the presidency, he said, "If that is true, he is the greatest man in history."

Question 3

How does the author show that George Washington is a great man?

- Ⓐ He led untrained soldiers into battle.
- Ⓑ He was unanimously elected president.
- Ⓒ He voluntarily gave up the power of the presidency.
- Ⓓ All of the above.

Question 4

Based upon the above story about George Washington, which of the following words best describe him?

- Ⓐ Smart
- Ⓑ Power hungry
- Ⓒ Strong leader
- Ⓓ Kind

Question 5

According to the text, why was Washington considered the most popular president?

- Ⓐ King George I said, "He is the greatest man in history."
- Ⓑ He was elected president by a unanimous vote.
- Ⓒ He wanted to be a powerful man and king.
- Ⓓ He was the first president

When Westinghouse, the inventor of the air brake, was working on his great invention, he made an application for a trial of his device to the New York Central Railroad. Vanderbilt the president of the railroad, thought the inventor's claims were absurd. In comparison with the hand brake then in use, Westinghouse stated that his brake could be operated by one man, instead of two, and that his brake would stop a fifty-car train in fifty yards, compared to a sixty-five car train in two hundred yards with hand brakes.

It is said that Vanderbilt roared with laughter. The idea of stopping a train of cars by wind appeared to him to be a joke. So he returned the letter, with these words scribbled at the bottom: "I have no time to waste on fools."

The young inventor next turned to the head of another railroad. He was younger and more progressive than his New York rival. He sent for Westinghouse, listened to his explanations, and even advanced him money to continue his experiments. Best of all, he tested the new brake and found that Westinghouse was on the right track. Vanderbilt, hearing of the test, regretted his curt dismissal of the idea. He wrote a courteous note to the inventor, fixing a time for an interview. The note came back with the brief inscription: "I have no time to waste on fools." George Westinghouse.

Question 6

Which of the following statements can be concluded after reading the passage above?

Ⓐ Westinghouse was thankful Vanderbilt helped him.
Ⓑ Vanderbilt regretted not listening to Westinghouse's ideas.
Ⓒ Westinghouse was a successful train engineer.
Ⓓ Westinghouse's invention was foolish.

Michael Jordan was the greatest basketball player of all time. When he played for the Chicago Bulls, they had one winning season after another. He scored more than 100 points in 1,108 games, won two Olympic gold medals, and was ranked #1 by ESPN Magazine. Chosen for the NBA All-Stars 14 times, Jordan was ten times the scoring champ, five times the Most Valuable Player, and six times the scoring champ of the NBA. When he began losing his hair, he shaved his head completely and started a fashion trend for other players. He was chosen to make an animated movie called "Space Jam" with Bugs Bunny. No other player has come close to those achievements.

Question 7

Which of the following is NOT a reason why Michael Jordan is considered the greatest basketball player of all time, according to the passage?

Ⓐ Michael Jordan shaved his head.
Ⓑ Michael Jordan won two gold medals in the Olympics.
Ⓒ Michael Jordan scored more than 100 points in 1,108 games.
Ⓓ Michael Jordan was the Most Valuable Player five times.

Question 8

Why did the author write this passage about Michael Jordan?

Ⓐ To tell about how Michael Jordan made a movie with Bugs Bunny.
Ⓑ To show what a great basketball player Michael Jordan is.
Ⓒ To give reader's Michael Jordan's life story.
Ⓓ To tell people what it is like to be a famous basketball player.

Most of the planets in our solar system have moons. Saturn has the most, with eighteen moons. Jupiter has sixteen, Uranus has fifteen. Earth has only one, but our moon has a big influence on the lives of humans on earth. In ancient times, people believed that moonlight could affect people's brains. The Latin word for moon was Luna. Words like "lunatic" and "looney" come from that idea. Many people still believe that more babies are born and more people die when the moon is full. Scientific studies that have been done to see whether the numbers of births and deaths actually increase when there is a full moon show that there is no increase. Gravitational pull from the moon affects the tides in the ocean, but does not seem to affect the births and deaths of people. Does the full moon cause people to fall in love? That's another question!

Question 9

What, according to the passage, has a "looney" effect on people?

Ⓐ The tides
Ⓑ Saturn
Ⓒ Babies
Ⓓ The moon

Question 10

After reading this passage, what inference can you make?

Ⓐ People believe the moon causes crazy things to happen.
Ⓑ Moonlight from the Earth's moon is less powerful because we only have one moon.
Ⓒ Births, deaths, and love can all happen because of our moon.
Ⓓ Earth's moon is bigger than Jupiter's.

Central Idea of Text (RI.6.2)

1. Books were hard to get for the mountain men among the western settlers.
2. Sometimes a mountain man would carry a single battered book with him for years.
3. Some of the men had Bibles, and even more had Shakespeare's plays.
4. Shakespeare was a favorite with mountain men, even if they could not read.
5. When they found someone who could read, he was often asked to read one of Shakespeare's plays to a group over a campfire.
6. There were mountain men who could not sign their own names, but could quote passages of Shakespeare by heart.

Question 1

Which sentence best shows the main idea of this paragraph?

Ⓐ Sentence #1
Ⓑ Sentence #6
Ⓒ Sentence #3
Ⓓ Sentence #5

Question 2

Which two sentences best support the main idea- that mountain men liked Shakespeare, even if they could not read?

Ⓐ Sentences #2 and #6
Ⓑ Sentences #3 and #5
Ⓒ Sentences #1 and #2
Ⓓ Sentences #3 and #6

Question 3

Which sentence does not directly support the main idea?

Ⓐ Sentence #2
Ⓑ Sentence #3
Ⓒ Sentence #5
Ⓓ Sentence #6

The rainforest has many layers. Different plants and animals live in each layer. Some layers get more sunlight than others.

Question 4

Which is the main idea of the passage?

Ⓐ We should take care of the rainforest.
Ⓑ There are many layers in the rainforest.
Ⓒ Some layers get sunlight.
Ⓓ Rainforests are too wet.

Question 5

A main idea is _____ and then has details that follow to support it.

Ⓐ Specific
Ⓑ General
Ⓒ Both specific and general
Ⓓ Very detailed

Question 6

The purpose of supporting details is _____.

Ⓐ To give you a conclusion
Ⓑ To tell you the point of view of the story
Ⓒ To tell the main idea
Ⓓ To give more information to support the main idea

Mike ran down the field dribbling the ball back and forth between his feet. Mike dodged the defensive player and kept moving down the field. Mike kicked the ball at the goal, but the goalie caught it right before it went in. Mike knew he would soon have time to try again

Question 7

What is the main idea of the passage?

Ⓐ Mike wants to learn to be faster on the field.
Ⓑ Mike wants to score a goal.
Ⓒ Mike wants to learn to kick the ball harder.
Ⓓ Mike dribbles the ball really well.

1. Homophones, homographs, and homonyms have different definitions.
2. Homophones are words that sound the same, but are spelled differently and have different meanings.
3. "The golfer drank tea before tee time."
4. Homographs are words that are spelled the same, but are not pronounced the same way.
5. "The artist is planning to record a new record."
6. When two homographs are also homophones, they are called homonyms: word pairs that are spelled the same and pronounced the same way.
7. "He felt fine after he paid the fine."
8. "You can drink juice from a can."
9. You can remember homographs by remembering that "graph" means to write, as in autograph.
10. You can remember homophones by remembering that "phone" means sound, as in telephone.

Question 8

Which sentence is the main idea of the passage?

Ⓐ Sentence #1
Ⓑ Sentence #4
Ⓒ Sentence #6
Ⓓ Sentence #10

Question 9

Which sentence is a supporting detail for Sentence #2?

Ⓐ Sentence #3
Ⓑ Sentence #4
Ⓒ Sentence #5
Ⓓ Sentence #10

Question 10

What sentence is supported by detail in Sentence #7?

Ⓐ Sentence #8
Ⓑ Sentence #6
Ⓒ Sentence #7
Ⓓ Sentence #5

Analyze how People, Events, or Ideas are Presented in Text (RI.6.3)

Everywhere around us there are millions of tiny living things called germs. They are so tiny that they can be seen only under the most powerful microscope. Some of these germs are no wider than twenty-five thousandths of an inch!

Louis Pasteur, the great French scientist, was the first to prove that germs exist. The germs in the air can be counted. The number of germs around us, especially in crowded rooms, is tremendous. Certain scientists counted 42,000 germs in approximately one cubic meter of air in a picture gallery when it was empty. But when the gallery was crowded with people, they found nearly 5,000,000 germs in the same place. In the open air germs are less abundant. There are fewer germs in country air than in town air. We see at once how important it is, therefore, to live as much as possible in the open air, and for the rooms we live in to always be well ventilated by fresh air.

Question 1

What is the main idea of the above passage?

Ⓐ Louis Pasteur was a great French scientist.
Ⓑ Germs are everywhere.
Ⓒ Germs are small.
Ⓓ Germs can be counted.

Question 2

Which of the following details does NOT support the main idea of the passage?

Ⓐ Germs are tiny and can only be seen using powerful microscopes.
Ⓑ There are fewer germs in open air.
Ⓒ The more people you are around the sicker you will become.
Ⓓ Germs are living things.

George Washington was the first and most popular U.S. President. He was the only one elected by a unanimous vote. It is often said of him that he was "first in war, first in peace and first in the hearts of his countrymen."

Washington led comparatively untrained and ill-equipped American soldiers to victory over the well-trained British in the Revolutionary War. As soon as the Constitution was ratified, he was chosen to be President.

Many of the generals who had fought under Washington did not believe that the 13 colonies could cooperate to form a single country without the strong leadership of a king. They approached him, saying that they would support him as King George I of the United States. Washington was dismayed at the idea, and asked the generals to promise never to mention it again. He served two terms as President and refused a third term, retiring to his farm in Virginia. When England's King George heard that Washington had voluntarily given up the power of the presidency, he said, "If that is true, he is the greatest man in history."

Question 3

What is the main idea of the above passage?

Ⓐ George Washington refused a third term as president.
Ⓑ King George said that Washington is a great man.
Ⓒ George Washington was also known as King George I of the United States.
Ⓓ George Washington was a great general and great first president.

When Michael Jordan played for the Chicago Bulls, they had one winning season after another. He scored more than 100 points in 1,108 games, won two Olympic gold medals, and was ranked #1 by ESPN Magazine. Chosen for the NBA All-Stars 14 times, Jordan was ten times the scoring champ, five times the Most Valuable Player, and six times the scoring champ of the NBA. When he began losing his hair, he shaved his head completely and started a fashion trend for other players. He was chosen to make an animated movie called "Space Jam" with Bugs Bunny. No other player has come close to those achievements.

Question 4

Which of the following would be the best introductory, or topic sentence, for the above passage?

Ⓐ Michael Jordan is often considered to be the greatest basketball player of all time.
Ⓑ Michael Jordan loves playing basketball.
Ⓒ When Michael Jackson isn't playing basketball he is staring in movies.
Ⓓ Michael Jackson won games, medals, and awards as a basketball player.

Question 5

Which of the following sentences best supports the main idea of the passage?

Ⓐ Michael Jordan was scoring champ of the NBA six times.
Ⓑ Michael Jordan scored more than 100 points in 1,108 games.
Ⓒ Michael Jordan is best friends with Bugs Bunny.
Ⓓ Both A and B.

When Westinghouse, the inventor of the air brake, was working on his great invention, he made an application for a trial of his device to the New York Central Railroad. Vanderbilt, the president of the railroad, thought the inventor's claims were absurd. In comparison with the hand brake then in use, Westinghouse stated that his brake could be operated by one man, instead of two, and that his brake would stop a fifty-car train in fifty yards, compared to a sixty-five car train in two hundred yards with hand brakes.

It is said that Vanderbilt roared with laughter. The idea of stopping a train of cars by wind appeared to him to be a joke. So he returned the letter, with these words scribbled at the bottom: "I have no time to waste on fools."

The young inventor next turned to the head of another railroad. He was younger and more progressive than his New York rival. He sent for Westinghouse, listened to his explanations, and even advanced him money to continue his experiments. Best of all, he tested the new brake and found that Westinghouse was on the right track. Vanderbilt, hearing of the test, regretted his curt dismissal of the idea. He wrote a courteous note to the inventor, fixing a time for an interview. The note came back with the brief inscription: "I have no time to waste on fools." George Westinghouse.

Question 6

What is the above passage about?

Ⓐ Railroads during the 1800s
Ⓑ Vanderbilt and his dislike for fools
Ⓒ Air brakes
Ⓓ George Westinghouse's invention

Question 7

How did Westinghouse react to Vanderbilt's dismissal of his idea?

Ⓐ Westinghouse gave up.
Ⓑ Westinghouse kept trying.
Ⓒ Westinghouse got mad at Vanderbilt.
Ⓓ Westinghouse decided to try inventing something else.

Question 8

What kind of person does the passage illustrate George Westinghouse to be?

Ⓐ Foolish
Ⓑ Smart
Ⓒ Determined
Ⓓ Courteous

Books were hard to get for the mountain men among the western settlers. Sometimes a mountain man would carry a single battered book with him for years. Some of the men had Bibles, and even more had Shakespeare's plays. Shakespeare was a favorite with mountain men, even if they could not read. When they found someone who could read, he was often asked to read one of Shakespeare's plays to a group over a campfire. There were mountain men who could not sign their own names, but could quote passages of Shakespeare by heart.

Question 9

How does the author of the above passage show that books were important to mountain men?

Ⓐ   Books were hard for mountain men to get.
Ⓑ   Some mountain men had Shakespeare's plays.
Ⓒ   Some mountain men could quote Shakespeare.
Ⓓ   Not all mountain men could read.

Washing clothes is a difficult task. The skill has to be learned and mastered. It is a tedious and tiresome process, which often discourages a person from going through the exercise. In spite of the availability of modern detergent powders, it remains a difficult task. An expert knows which parts of the dress need special care and attention. The collars of shirts and the seat and pockets of pants are generally dirtier than the other parts. But to wash well, what you require most is patience and the knowledge of the texture and quality of the cloth you are washing so that you can differentiate between clothes which can be put in warm water and clothes which must never be washed in hot water. Woolens, silk and cotton clothes need different types of washing and detergents. One must have proper knowledge of these before washing clothes.

Question 10

How does the author of the above passage illustrate that washing clothes is a difficult task?

Ⓐ   By discussing the different types of washing machines.
Ⓑ   By pointing out that certain parts of clothing need special care and attention.
Ⓒ   By talking about all the different laundry detergent options.
Ⓓ   By explaining how time consuming laundry can be.

Determine Technical Meanings (RI.6.4)

Question 1

What is a synonym of a word?

Ⓐ A word that has the same meaning as the given word.
Ⓑ A word that has the opposite meaning of a given word.
Ⓒ A word that has the same spelling as the given word.
Ⓓ A word that has the same pronunciation as the given word.

Question 2

Which of the following statements is true about antonyms?

Ⓐ They have the same meaning as the given word.
Ⓑ They are the definitions of a given word.
Ⓒ They have the same sounds as a given word.
Ⓓ They are the opposites of a given word.

Question 3

The words "minute" (time) and "minute" (extremely small) are pronounced differently and have different meanings.

These types of words are called _____.

Ⓐ Homophones
Ⓑ Homonyms
Ⓒ Homographs
Ⓓ Homo-words

Question 4

Which of the choices below is an example of an antonym?

Ⓐ Clever, crazy
Ⓑ Pretty, beautiful
Ⓒ Narrow, skinny
Ⓓ Abundant, scarce

Question 5

Which of the choices below is an example of synonyms?

Ⓐ mini, tiny
Ⓑ clever, foolish
Ⓒ good, bad
Ⓓ soggy, dry

Question 6

United States. Preamble and First Amendment to the United States Constitution. (1787, 1791) Preamble We, the People of the United States, in Order to form a more perfect Union, establish Justice, insure domestic Tranquility, provide for the common defence, pro- mote the general Welfare, and secure the Blessings of Liberty to ourselves and our Posterity, do ordain and establish this Constitution of the United States of America. Amendment I Congress shall make no law respecting the establishment of religion, or prohibiting the free exercise thereof; or abridging the freedom of speech, or of the press; or the right of people peaceably to assemble, and to petition the Government for a redress of grievances.

What is the meaning of the word welfare as it is used in the passage?

Ⓐ concern of the government for its citizens' health, safety, and peace
Ⓑ concern of the government for where people will get money
Ⓒ concern of the government for where people will get food
Ⓓ concern of the government for its citizens' ability to take care of themselves

Question 7

What is the meaning of the phrase domestic tranquility as it is used in the passage?

Ⓐ peace in the house
Ⓑ peace in the country
Ⓒ peace in other countries
Ⓓ peace in warring countries

Question 8

What is the meaning of the word posterity as it is used in the passage?

Ⓐ others in this generation
Ⓑ the backside of an event
Ⓒ an individual's future
Ⓓ future generations

Question 9

Which of the following statements defines homophones?

Ⓐ The words that have the same meaning and different spellings.
Ⓑ The words that have the same sound but different meanings.
Ⓒ The words that have the same sound but have different meanings and spellings.
Ⓓ The words that do not have the same sound but have the same meaning andspelling.

Question 10

Identify the correct set of homophones from the following.

Ⓐ mustard, mustered
Ⓑ loan, lone
Ⓒ lumbar, lumber
Ⓓ both A and B

Structure of Text (RI.6.5)

Question 1

Identify where the underlined sentence below belongs in the paragraph.

Start with the freshest bread you can find.

I will tell you how to make a perfect peanut butter sandwich.
Take the two pieces of bread.
Add a good-sized scoop of crunchy peanut butter, and be sure to spread it on both pieces of bread. Find a jar of your favorite jam.
Use slightly less jam than peanut butter, and spread it on only one slice of bread.
Put the two slices together and cut the sandwich in half. Enjoy.

- Ⓐ The missing sentence should be first.
- Ⓑ The missing sentence should be second.
- Ⓒ The missing sentence should be third.
- Ⓓ The missing sentence should be fourth.

Question 2

Identify where the underlined sentence below belongs in the paragraph.

During the pre-competition phase, continue the aerobic training, but add strength training and sprints.

Training for tennis can be broken down into four phases.
During the preparation phase, work on aerobic fitness with jogging, swimming, or cycling as you train heavily on the specifics of tennis.
While competing, training can ease up except for the specifics of tennis.
For several weeks after competition, rest from playing tennis but keep up your fitness by playing other sports.

- Ⓐ The missing sentence should be first.
- Ⓑ The missing sentence should be second.
- Ⓒ The missing sentence should be third.
- Ⓓ The missing sentence should be fourth.

Question 3

Identify where the underlined sentence below belongs in the paragraph.

In French, the word means "rotten pot."

Today we have spray cans for freshening the air, but it's more fun to make a potpourri. Potpourris were originally made in France by creating a mixture of flower petals and leaves that was allowed to sit in a crock for months. Today, many people still like to make potpourris from herbs and flowers. You can make your own from herbs and flowers from the garden.

Ⓐ The missing sentence should be first.
Ⓑ The missing sentence should be second.
Ⓒ The missing sentence should be third.
Ⓓ The missing sentence should be fourth.

Question 4

Arrange the sentences below in the most logical order.

1. On the front of each cap is a white horse.
2. The caps also have the motto, "They fear no difficulty."
3. Officers can be identified by the crimson sash worn over their shoulders.
4. The tallest men have high bearskin caps.
5. The British troops present a colorful appearance.
6. Crowds gather to watch the elegant soldiers parade by.

Ⓐ 6, 1, 2, 5, 4, 3
Ⓑ 5, 3, 4, 1, 2, 6
Ⓒ 5, 6, 3, 4, 1, 2
Ⓓ Both 'B' or 'C'

Question 5

Arrange the sentences in the most logical order.

1. Most farm families raised geese, so goose feathers were plentiful.
2. Colonists also used the feathers of wild turkeys and hawks.
3. Crow feathers were harder to collect, but were considered the best for making fine lines.
4. Colonists often made their quill pens from goose feathers.

Ⓐ 4, 1, 2, 3
Ⓑ 1, 2, 3, 4
Ⓒ 3, 2, 1, 4
Ⓓ 2, 3, 1, 4

Question 6

Arrange the sentences in the most logical order.

1. Later, European traders spread pineapple growing to Africa and the Pacific Islands, including Hawaii.
2. The name was later changed to pineapple.
3. The name may come from the Dutch word for pinecone, which is pi jnappel.
4. Christopher Columbus was the first European to taste what he called "Indian pinecones."

Ⓐ 4, 3, 2, 1
Ⓑ 4, 1, 3, 4
Ⓒ 1, 2, 3, 4
Ⓓ 3, 2, 1, 4

When Westinghouse, the inventor of the air brake, was working on his great invention, he made an application for a trial of his device to the New York Central Railroad. Vanderbilt, the president of the railroad, thought the inventor's claims were absurd. In comparison with the hand brake then in use, Westinghouse stated that his brake could be operated by one man, instead of two, and that his brake would stop a fifty-car train in fifty yards, compared to a sixty-five car train in two hundred yards with hand brakes.

It is said that Vanderbilt roared with laughter. The idea of stopping a train of cars by wind appeared to him to be a joke. So he returned the letter, with these words scribbled at the bottom: "I have no time to waste on fools."

The young inventor next turned to the head of another railroad. He was younger and more progressive than his New York rival. He sent for Westinghouse, listened to his explanations, and even advanced him money to continue his experiments. Best of all, he tested the new brake and found that Westinghouse was on the right track. Vanderbilt, hearing of the test, regretted his curt dismissal of the idea. He wrote a courteous note to the inventor, fixing a time for an interview. The note came back with the brief inscription: "I have no time to waste on fools." George Westinghouse.

Question 7

What kind of a writing piece is the above passage?

Ⓐ A personal narrative
Ⓑ A persuasive essay
Ⓒ An informative/expository passage
Ⓓ A journal entry

Question 8

Which of following would turn the above passage into a personal narrative?

Ⓐ If the above passage was written by Westinghouse himself.
Ⓑ If the author was President Vanderbilt and he wrote about George Westinghouse.
Ⓒ If the author was a third person.
Ⓓ None of the above

Question 9

What are the main parts of an essay?

Ⓐ A topic title
Ⓑ An introduction to the topic
Ⓒ Details about the topic and a conclusion to the topic
Ⓓ All of the above

Question 10

What are the parts of a business letter?

Ⓐ The heading, the inside address
Ⓑ The greeting, the body
Ⓒ The complimentary close, the signature line
Ⓓ All of the above

Determine Author's Point of View (RI.6.6)

Dogs are better pets than cats for many reasons. Dogs are a man's best friend and can learn tricks. Dogs will get you things when you ask them to. Dogs will go walking or running with you to help keep you in shape. Dogs like to cuddle and protect their owners.

Question 1

What is the purpose of the above passage?

Ⓐ To inform
Ⓑ To explain
Ⓒ To persuade
Ⓓ To entertain

If you invent a new word and enough people like it, you may find it in the dictionary. Dictionaries add new words as they come into common use. The fancy word for a brand-new word is "neologism." In 2011, the Merriam-Webster Collegiate Dictionary added some neologisms you probably know, such as "tweet," "fist bump," and "social media."

Some of the new words may not be so familiar.

• "Planking" is a game of lying face down, hands at your sides, in the most unusual place you can think of, and having your picture taken and posted on the internet.
• A "bromance" is a close friendship – but not a romance – between two men.
• A "robocall" is a call made automatically by a machine repeating a taped message.
• A "helicopter parent" is one who hovers over their children, becoming much too involved in their lives.
• And "crowdsourcing"? That's the way many people can each do a little bit of a very large project. The country of Iceland, for example, is crowdsourcing a new constitution for their country, so if you have an idea about what they ought to include, you can go online and send them your suggestion.

At the same time new words are being added, old words that are no longer widely recognized are dropped from the dictionary. This year, the dictionary deleted the words "growlery" (a room where you can go to complain) and "brabble" (another word for squabble). If you haven't heard those words before, you probably won't miss them!

Question 2

What is the purpose of the passage above?

Ⓐ To inform
Ⓑ To explain
Ⓒ To persuade
Ⓓ To entertain

I will tell you how to make a perfect peanut butter sandwich. Start with the freshest bread you can find. Take two pieces of bread. Add a good-sized scoop of crunchy peanut butter, and be sure to spread it on both pieces of bread. Find a jar of your favorite jam. Use slightly less jam than peanut butter, and spread it on only one slice of bread. Put the two slices together and cut the sandwich in half. Enjoy.

Question 3

What is the purpose of the passage above?

Ⓐ To inform
Ⓑ To explain
Ⓒ To persuade
Ⓓ To entertain

Everywhere around us there are millions of tiny living things called germs. They are so tiny that they can be seen only under the most powerful microscope. Some of these germs are no wider than twenty-five thousandths of an inch!

Louis Pasteur, the great French scientist, was the first to prove that germs exist. The germs in the air can be counted. The number of germs around us, especially in crowded rooms, is tremendous. Certain scientists counted 42,000 germs in approximately one cubic meter of air in a picture gallery when it was empty. But when the gallery was crowded with people they found nearly 5,000,000 germs in the same place. In the open air germs are less abundant. There are fewer germs in country air than in town air. We see at once how important it is, therefore, to live as much as possible in the open air, and for the rooms we live in to always be well ventilated by fresh air.

Question 4

What is the purpose of the passage above?

Ⓐ To inform
Ⓑ To explain
Ⓒ To persuade
Ⓓ To entertain

Football is the most exciting sport. During a football game, two teams of eleven players battle to reach the end zone. During the game, the players try to catch or run with the ball without being tackled by the opposing team. Sometimes players jump over each other, break tackles, and run as fast as lightning. Football fans cheer extremely loud when their team reaches the end zone. There is never a dull moment in football.

Question 5

What is the purpose of the passage above?

Ⓐ To convince readers to go to a football game.
Ⓑ To tell a story about what happened at a football game.
Ⓒ To explain to readers about what happens at a football game.
Ⓓ To help the reader understand why to never attend a football game.

Eating carrots, broccoli and string beans are good for you. Making sure to have healthy vegetables in your diet is important. Some people think eating vegetables at one meal is good enough, but it isn't; you should eat vegetables at least 3 meals a day.

Question 6

What is the purpose of the passage above?

Ⓐ To convince the reader to eat more vegetables.
Ⓑ To give information about different types of vegetables.
Ⓒ To tell about a cartoon where the characters are played by vegetables.
Ⓓ The help the reader understand there is nothing important about vegetables.

The sky was dark and overcast. It had been raining all night long and there was no sign of it stopping. I thought that my Sunday would be ruined. As it poured outside, I settled down by the window to watch the rain. The park opposite my house looked even more green and fresh than usual. The branches of the tall trees swayed so hard in the strong wind that I thought they would break. A few children were splashing about in the mud puddles and having a wonderful time. I wished I could join them too! There were very few people out on the road and those who were hurried on their way, wrapped in raincoats and carrying umbrellas.

My mother announced that lunch was ready. It was piping hot and very welcoming in the damp weather. We spent the afternoon listening to music and to the downpour outside.

In the evening we chatted and made paper boats that were meant to sail in the stream of water outside. It was not a bad day after all!

Question 7

What point of view is the story above told from?

Ⓐ First person
Ⓑ Second person
Ⓒ Third person
Ⓓ Fourth person

Once upon a time four boys lived in the countryside. One boy was very clever but he did not like books. His name was Good Sense. The other boys were not very clever but they read every book in the school. When they became grown men, they decided to go out into the world to earn their livelihood.

They left home and came to a forest where they halted for the night. When they woke up in the morning, they found the bones of a lion. Three of them, who had learnt their books well at school, decided to make a lion out of the bones.

Good Sense told them, "A lion is a dangerous animal. It will kill us. Don't make a lion." But the three disregarded his advice and started making a lion. Good Sense was very clever. When his friends were busy making the lion, he climbed up a tree to save himself. No sooner had the three young men created the lion and gave it life, than it pounced upon them and ate them up. Good Sense climbed down the tree and went home very sadly.

Question 8

What point of view is the story above told from?

Ⓐ First person
Ⓑ Second person
Ⓒ Third person
Ⓓ Fourth person

This is how to make a perfect peanut butter sandwich. Start with the freshest bread you can find. Take the two pieces of bread. Add a good-sized scoop of crunchy peanut butter, and be sure to spread it on both pieces of bread. Find a jar of your favorite jam. Use slightly less jam than peanut butter, and spread it on only one slice of bread. Put the two slices together and cut the sandwich in half. Enjoy.

Question 9

What point of view is the story above told from?

Ⓐ First person
Ⓑ Second person
Ⓒ Third person
Ⓓ Fourth person

Most of the planets in our solar system have moons. Saturn has the most, with eighteen moons. Jupiter has sixteen, Uranus has fifteen. Earth has only one, but our moon has a big influence on the lives of humans on earth. In ancient times, people believed that moonlight could affect people's brains. The Latin word for moon was Luna. Words like "lunatic" and "looney" come from that idea. Many people still believe that more babies are born and more people die when the moon is full. Scientific studies that have been done to see whether the numbers of births and deaths actually increase when there is a full moon show that there is no increase. Gravitational pull from the moon affects the tides in the ocean, but does not seem to affect the births and deaths of people. Does the full moon cause people to fall in love? That's another question!

Question 10

What point of view is the story above told from?

Ⓐ First person
Ⓑ Second person
Ⓒ Third person
Ⓓ Fourth person

Integration of Knowledge and Ideas

Evaluating Arguments in Text (RI.6.8)

Michael Jordan was the greatest basketball player of all time. He scored more than 100 points in 1,108 games, won two Olympic gold medals, and was ranked #1 by ESPN Magazine. Chosen for the NBA All-Stars 14 times, Jordan was ten times the scoring champ, five times the Most Valuable Player, and six times the scoring champ of the NBA. No other player has come close to those achievements.

Question 1

Identify the main idea – the claim – in the above persuasive paragraph.
_____.

Ⓐ Jordan was six times the 'scoring champ' for NBA.
Ⓑ Jordan was chosen for the NBA All-Stars 14 times.
Ⓒ The claim is that Jordan was the greatest basketball player.
Ⓓ Jordan was a basketball player.

Michael Jordan was the greatest basketball player of all time. When he played for the Chicago Bulls, they had one winning season after another. When he began losing his hair, he shaved his head completely and started a fashion trend for other players. He was chosen to make an animated movie called "Space Jam" with Bugs Bunny. There are many good players, but Michael Jordan will always be my favorite.

Question 2

The claim: Jordan was the greatest basketball player.
Details to support this claim include:_____.

Ⓐ He was the best player on the team.
Ⓑ When he began losing his hair, he shaved his head completely and started a fashion trend for other players.
Ⓒ He was chosen to make an animated movie called "Space Jam" with Bugs Bunny.
Ⓓ When he played for the Chicago Bulls, they had one winning season after an other.

Life in the city is always exciting. There are more than a million people in the city where I live. There are street fairs and sidewalk vendors downtown. Most days, people are going about their daily business, just working. In that way, a big city is no different from a small town. But in the city, there are many more concerts, lectures, theatrical performances, and other kinds of entertainment. Most of those things are expensive and I can't afford to go. Because of the curfew, young people aren't allowed on the streets at night, and I usually have a lot of homework.

Question 3

Why would I like to live in a city?

Select the answer with the best arguments to support the above sentence:

Ⓐ 1. City life is always exciting.
    2. There are one million people living in the city.
Ⓑ 1. There are street fairs and sidewalk vendors.
    2. There are concerts and all kinds of entertainment.
Ⓒ 1. Young people aren't allowed on the streets at night.
    2. I have a lot of homework.
Ⓓ 1. Most of the things are expensive.
    2. I can't afford to go to these exciting places.

Question 4

Why can't young people enjoy city life?

Select the answer with the best arguments to support the above sentence:

Ⓐ 1. City life is always exciting.
    2. Too many people live in the city.
Ⓑ 1. There are street fairs and sidewalk vendors.
    2. There are concerts and all kinds of entertainment.
Ⓒ 1. There's a curfew for young people at night.
    2. Young people have no time due to too much homework.
Ⓓ 1. People go about their daily work.
    2. A big city is actually no different from a small town.

Fast food is unhealthy; it leads to obesity and disease, but the convenience and addictiveness of it contributes to the laziness of the general population. Most people eat fast food because they lack the time to prepare a more nutritious meal. It seems as though there is a fast food restaurant on every street corner. The general population overlooks the fact that eating nothing but these greasy foods will contribute to weight gain. Fast food is addictive because it is easily accessible and tastes so good.

Question 5

In the above passage, which sentence supports the argument that fast food contributes to unhealthy weight gain?

Ⓐ Most people eat fast food because they lack the time to prepare a more nutritious meal.
Ⓑ It seems as though there is a fast food restaurant on every street corner.
Ⓒ The general population overlooks the fact that eating nothing but these greasy foods will cause you to gain weight.
Ⓓ Fast food is addictive for the convenience of it.

Kickboxing is a great form of exercise. This type of exercise tones your entire body. Punching a bag helps you gain strength and muscle in your arms. You also use the bag to do different types of kicks, thus strengthening your legs as well. Kickboxing is an overall body workout that everyone should try.

Question 6

The claim: Kickboxing is a great form of exercise.
Select the answer that most completely supports the claim:_____

Ⓐ This exercise routine allows you to use a punching bag.
Ⓑ This exercise strengthens your muscles.
Ⓒ This type of exercise tones your entire body.
Ⓓ Kickboxing is the new trend in exercise routines.

Electric cars are a new innovative type of car that helps the environment. They use little to no gas, therefore keeping pollutants out of the air. They may be a little more expensive than the average car, but you will make that money back in savings on gas. The electric car is now being made by almost all car companies.

Question 7

The claim: Electric cars are a new innovative type of car.
Details to support the claim include: _____

Ⓐ Electric cars are a great way to help the environment.
Ⓑ Electric cars are only a few years old.
Ⓒ Electric cars are expensive.
Ⓓ Most companies are now making electric cars.

Running a marathon is a great accomplishment. Training for a marathon takes months. First, you have to start running short distances, and increase each week the distance you run. During your training, you will eventually start running 20 miles at a time. A full marathon is 26.2 miles and very hard for people to finish. With a little time, training, and hard work, anyone can run a marathon. Completing the marathon is a great accomplishment because it shows excellent dedication and athletic ability.

Question 8

Identify the claim in this passage.

Ⓐ Running a marathon requires you to train a lot.
Ⓑ Running a marathon is a great accomplishment.
Ⓒ Running requires excellent dedication.
Ⓓ Not many people are able to complete a marathon.

Smart phones are the newest innovative technology out there. On the Smart phone you can video chat with your friends or family members to keep in touch. Smart phones also are a great way to stay organized and keep your life on track. Smart phones are an easy way to search the internet when you are out and need to find something quickly. They allow you to access tons of information.

Question 9

Identify the claim in this passage.

Ⓐ Smart phones are the newest innovative technology out there.
Ⓑ Smart phones are the best phone out there.
Ⓒ Smart phones are the best way to stay organized.
Ⓓ Smart phones can be used for video chatting.

Horses are used for many different types of activities. Horses can be used to pull carts. They are also used for riding English style in which the rider can jump and show them. Horses can also be used for riding Western style in which riders can herd and rope cattle and go on trail rides. An English style rider can also perform dressage, which is a highly precise series of movements involving the rider and the horse.

Question 10

Identify the claim in this paragraph.

Ⓐ Dressage is the most intricate form of horse training.
Ⓑ Horses can be used for many different activities.
Ⓒ Horses can be ridden English style.
Ⓓ Horses can be ridden Western style.

Compare/Contrast One Author's Presentation with Another (RI.6.9)

"Peace cannot be achieved through violence, it can only be attained through understanding." Ralph Waldo Emerson

"Peace cannot be kept by force; it can only be achieved by understanding." Albert Einstein

Question 1

What do both of these individuals say about peace?

Ⓐ   You can only have peace by fighting.
Ⓑ   You can only have peace through understanding.
Ⓒ   You can only have peace when everyone gets along.
Ⓓ   Peace is all around us.

"Music is a world within itself, with a language we all understand." Stevie Wonder

"Without music, life would be a mistake." Fredrich Nietzsche

Question 2

What is similar about these to quotations?

Ⓐ   Both talk about languages.
Ⓑ   Both talk about life.
Ⓒ   Both talk about music.
Ⓓ   They have nothing similar.

Question 3

Which one of the answers below is a great way to visually compare and contrast information?

Ⓐ   Venn Diagram
Ⓑ   Chart
Ⓒ   Graph
Ⓓ   All of the above

Question 4

To compare and contrast means _____

- Ⓐ Explain the details about two things
- Ⓑ Explain how two things are different
- Ⓒ Explain how two things are alike
- Ⓓ Explain how two things are alike and different

Question 5

Lakes and ponds are similar because _____.

- Ⓐ They are saltwater
- Ⓑ You can fish in them
- Ⓒ You can jet ski in them
- Ⓓ You can sail in them

Question 6

Snowfall and rainfall are similar; Which of the following is true with both of these?

- Ⓐ Wet drops that accumulate on the ground and cause hazardous driving conditions.
- Ⓑ Large drops that are white and clear.
- Ⓒ Wet drops that turn to ice.
- Ⓓ Wet drops that disappear when they touch the ground.

Read the quotations and then answer the question that follows.

1. "For every disciplined effort there is a multiple reward." - Jim Rohn

2. "Genius is one percent inspiration and ninety-nine percent perspiration." - Thomas Alva Edison

Question 7

Both Edison and Rohn are talking about the benefit of _____.

- Ⓐ genius
- Ⓑ reward
- Ⓒ effort
- Ⓓ inspiration

"Friendship is not something you learn in school. But if you haven't learned the meaning of friendship, you really haven't learned anything." Muhammad Ali

"If you live to be 100, I hope to live to be 100 minus 1 day, so I never have to live without you." Winnie the Pooh

Question 8

What do both of these quotations have in common?

Ⓐ They are both about living life.
Ⓑ They are both about friendship.
Ⓒ They are both about learning.
Ⓓ They have nothing in common

Question 9

Read the quotations and then answer the question that follows.

"Education is the most powerful weapon which you can use to change the world." Nelson Mandela

"Be the change you wish to see in the world." Gandhi

Both of these quotations talk about changing the world. What two contrasting things do they say makes change in the world?

Ⓐ Education, yourself
Ⓑ Weapons, yourself
Ⓒ Yourself, man
Ⓓ Education; weapons

Question 10

The desert is hot and dry whereas the _____ are cold and icy.

Ⓐ Mountains
Ⓑ Forests
Ⓒ Tropical islands
Ⓓ Polar regions

End of Reading: Informational Text

Answer Key and Detailed Explanations

Reading: Informational Text

Cite Textual Evidence (RI.6.1)

Question No.	Answer	Detailed Explanations
1	A	The text specifically states that an empty gallery had 42,000 germs but when filled with people, that same gallery had nearly 5,000,000 germs. One can then conclude that a crowded space will hold more germs. The correct answer is A.
2	D	While Louis Pasteur discovered germs there is no evidence in the story to support that he liked counting germs. Yes, germs are too small to be seen with the naked eye but they can be seen using powerful microscopes. Even though people do carry germs, the best concluding statement from this passage would be that there are fewer germs in fresh air. The correct answer is D.
3	D	Throughout the passage, each of the options is pointed out as something significant George Washington did in order to make him a great man. One can draw the conclusion that each factor makes him a great man.
4	C	The text implies that George Washington was not interested in being powerful; therefore Answer B would not be a correct choice. There is no evidence within the text that either supports or disputes that George Washington was a kind man. While his actions certainly showed that he was a smart man, the fact that George Washington was a strong leader is implied in how he led his army as well as knowing when it was his time to share the power by leaving office
5	B	At the beginning of the passage, the text not only states that George Washington is the most popular president but also specifically states that he was elected by a unanimous vote which means that everyone voted for him thus giving him the popular vote.
6	B	In the last paragraph, the passage states that Vanderbilt regretted dismissing Westinghouse's idea of an air brake. As a result, one can conclude that Vanderbilt regretted not taking the time to hear about Westinghouse's invention. The correct answer is B.

Question No.	Answer	Detailed Explanations
7	A	While it is true that Michael Jordan did shave his head, it does not support the idea that he is the greatest basketball player of all time; whereas all the other statements do support this idea. The correct answer is A.
8	B	While Michael Jordan did star in a movie with Bugs Bunny, this is not the most significant part of the passage. Yes, it tells a little about Michael Jordan's life but it is not his life story, it is merely highlights of his career as a famous basketball player. Since the passage tells primarily about Michael Jordan as a basketball player and all he has accomplished, it can be concluded that the author wrote the passage to show what a great basketball player he is. The correct answer is B.
9	D	The passage specifically states that our moon is thought to influence the lives of humans. Therefore, the correct answer is D.
10	A	There is no evidence in the passage which shows that either our moon is less powerful because we only have one or that our moon is bigger than Jupiter's. The text does suggest that people believe the moon causes crazy things to happen like more births, deaths, and people falling in love but there is no proof these things happen. The only thing the passage says for sure, is that people do believe that "looney" things happen and since looney is a synonym for crazy, the correct answer is A.

Central Idea of Text (RI.6.2)

Question No.	Answer	Detailed Explanations
1	B	The main idea is that mountain men liked Shakespeare, even if they could not read. Sentence six exemplifies this idea the most.
2	D	More men had Shakespeare than the Bible, and they memorized Shakespeare. That shows how much they loved it.
3	A	The fact that mountain men carried books around for years does not directly prove that they liked Shakespeare best.
4	B	The only answer that is a clear main idea is answer choice B. Option C is a supporting detail. Options A and D are not mentioned.
5	B	Main ideas are general. If a statement is too specific, then it might be a supporting detail and not the main idea.
6	D	The main idea of a passage is supported by details that follow it. That's why the answer is D.
7	B	Mike missed and he wants to try again. He really wants to score a goal for his team, so B is the answer
8	A	If you looked first at Sentences #1 and #10, you were checking wisely. The main idea of a paragraph is often the first or the last sentence. In this case, Sentence #10 is a supporting detail, and Sentence #1 is the main idea.
9	A	If you looked first at Sentence #3 and then chose A, you made the right decision. Supporting details generally follow the idea they're supporting.
10	B	If you selected B, Sentence #6, you made the right choice. The supporting details often follow immediately the sentence they support.

Analyze how People, Events or Ideas are Presented in Text (RI.6.3)

Question No.	Answer	Detailed Explanations
1	B	Answer choices A, C, and D present minor details related to the bigger, overall topic that germs are everywhere. The correct answer is B.
2	C	Answer choice C is the only answer that is not even presented in the story; therefore it is not a supporting detail. The correct answer is C.
3	D	Answers A and B both provide supporting details. Answer choice C is a misinterpretation of the text. Answer choice D presents what the passage is about – George Washington was a great general and president.
4	A	The only answer choice which completely identifies who Michael Jordan is and why is answer choice A. This would make the best, broad introductory sentence.
5	D	Both answer choices A and B support the main idea of the passage that Michael Jordan is a great basketball player. Answer choice C does not support the main idea. The correct answer choice is D.
6	D	While the passage does talk about the railroads, Vanderbilt, and air brakes, it is actually about George Westinghouse's invention of the air brake. The correct answer is D.
7	B	Even though Vanderbilt felt Westinghouse was a fool, Westinghouse kept trying. The passage specifically states that Westinghouse went on to try another railroad that listened to his ideas and tested his air brake. The correct answer is B.
8	C	While the fact that Westinghouse invented something very important, the air brake, shows that he is smart and he did demonstrate that he is courteous in his interactions with Vanderbilt, he is best described as determined because he did not give up. Only Vanderbilt described Westinghouse as foolish. The correct answer is C.
9	A	While each of the answer choices are true, only answer choice A illustrates how books were important to mountain men and that was because they were hard to get.
10	B	The author specifically states that certain parts of clothing or dress need special attention or care. The author then goes on to support this idea. The correct answer choice is B.

Determine Technical Meanings (RI.6.4)

Question No.	Answer	Detailed Explanations
1	A	Answer A is correct because synonyms will basically have the same definition as the original word they are representing.
2	D	The words will have completely opposite meanings, so the answer is D.
3	C	The answer is C because "minute" (time) and "minute" (extremely small) are example of homographs, words that are spelled the same but have different pronunciations and meanings.
4	D	Answer choice D is correct because those two words are complete opposites.
5	A	Answer choice A contains the synonym. The other answer choices are antonyms.
6	A	Though the word welfare has many meanings, in this case, the technical meaning is the concern of the government for the health, safety, peace, and morality of its citizens.
7	B	Although domestic can sometimes mean house, when read in context, the phrase can be seen as a reference to the entire country. In this case, domestic means home front, or country, and tranquility means peace.
8	D	Though posterity has several meanings, the technical meaning in this passage is referring to current generations.
9	C	Answer choice C is correct because that is the exact definition of a homophone.
10	D	Answer choices A and B both have words that sound the same but are spelled differently and have different meanings. For that reason, the correct answer is D.

Structure of Text (RI.6.5)

Question No.	Answer	Detailed Explanations
1	B	If you chose B, the missing sentence should be second, you made the best choice. Although it says "Start," you cannot start until you know what you are starting to do, so the missing sentence should not be first. You should select the freshest bread before you take the pieces of it, so the missing sentence should not be third, and it would not make sense in the fourth position.
2	C	If you chose C, the missing sentence should be third, you picked the right answer. The phrase, "continue the aerobic training" lets you know that aerobic training had to have already begun at some point, and it is mentioned in the second sentence.
3	C	If you chose C, the missing sentence should be third, you picked the best response. The definition of potpourri should come after it is mentioned that they were originally made in France, and that the flowers and leaves sat for months.
4	D	If you chose D, you made a good decision. Either one of these arrangements would be a good sequence for the sentences.
5	A	If you picked A, you made the best choice. If the paragraph doesn't begin with sentence 4, the reader will not know what the paragraph is talking about, and sentence 4 is only offered once as the first choice.
6	A	If you put the paragraph in reverse order, it reads perfectly. That is why A is the correct answer.
7	C	This piece gives information, so answer choice C is correct.
8	A	If the paper were written by Westinghouse about his experience, then it would be a personal narrative.
9	D	All of the above mentioned things are part of an essay. Answer choice D is correct.
10	D	All of these things are part of a business letter.

Determine Author's Point of View (RI.6.6)

Question No.	Answer	Detailed Explanations
1	C	The passage is trying to persuade the reader as to why dogs are better pets than cats. The correct answer is C.
2	A	The passage is giving information on how words are added to or deleted from the dictionary. The correct answer is A.
3	B	The passage is explaining how to make a peanut butter and jelly sandwich. The correct answer is C.
4	A	The passage is giving information about germs. The correct answer is A.
5	C	While the passage says that football is an exciting sport and that there is never a dull moment, the author does not use persuasive language aimed at convincing the reader. Also, the passage does not tell a story. It does, however, tell about what happens at a game. The correct answer is C.
6	A	The passage ends by saying "you should eat vegetables at least 3 meals a day." It also gives information to backup why this is important. Therefore, the passage is trying to convince readers to eat more vegetables. The correct answer is A.
7	A	Since the story uses the word "I" it must be told from first person point of view. The correct answer is A.
8	C	Since the story is told from the perspective of a narrator, without using "I", it is told from third person point of view.
9	B	The passage about is giving directions with no narrator, therefore it is told from second person point of view.
10	C	Since the passage is providing factual information, it is told from third person point of view.

Evaluating Arguments in Text (RI.6.8)

Question No.	Answer	Detailed Explanations
1	C	All of the evidence in the passage points to the fact that Jordan was a truly great basketball player. That is why the main idea can be found in answer choice C.
2	D	It was not mentioned in the passage that he was the best player on the team. The only detail that supports the main idea is D, he contributed to many of the Bulls' wins.
3	B	Answer choice B contains two positive things about living in the city. Those are the two sentences that support why the author likes living in the city.
4	C	Answer choice C gives two reasons why young people can't enjoy city life. The other answers do not contain relevant arguments.
5	C	Answer choice C is the only one that mentions gaining weight, and the other answers do not support the argument listed above.
6	C	Answer choice C is the one that most completely goes with the claim that kickboxing is a great form of exercise. Every exercise strengthens the muscles, and it does not mention in the article anything about it being a new trend. It does mention a punching bag, but that is only one part of kickboxing.
7	A	Although all of the answers contain true statements, only answer choice A supports the claim that the cars are innovative in that they are good for the environment.
8	B	The claim, or controlling idea, is usually at the beginning of the paragraph. That is true in this case. The answer is B because that's what the first sentence says.
9	A	The opening sentence is the claim, or the controlling idea. The other 3 answer choices are opinions and details, not the main claim of the paragraph.
10	B	The claim in this paragraph is the main idea, or controlling idea. It's what the author is trying to convince you of. Answer choice B contains the claim of this passage.

Compare/Contrast One Author's Presentation with Another (RI.6.9)

Question No.	Answer	Detailed Explanations
1	B	Both men are talking about how peace can only be attained through non-violence and understanding. The correct answer is B.
2	C	Both quotations, while having a different message, speak about the importance and value of music. The correct answer choice is C.
3	D	You can use all of the above to effectively compare and contrast.
4	D	Comparing is seeing how things are alike and contrasting is seeing how they are different. For that reason, the answer is D.
5	B	Ponds are not big enough to jet ski or sail in, and ponds and lakes are fresh water bodies of water. The only thing answer that is true is B.
6	A	Answer choice A is the only one that describes both rain and snow. The other answers only describe one, either rain or snow.
7	C	Both quotes are about effort, so the correct answer is C.
8	B	Both of these quotes are about friendship even if it is not specifically stated. The correct answer is B.
9	A	While both quotes talk about changing the world, the first quote stresses that education leads to change whereas the second quote suggests that you yourself create change. The correct answer is A.
10	D	Polar regions are the only logical answer because they are cold and icy. The correct answer is D.

Language
Conventions of Standard English

Question 1

Identify the adjective in the following sentence.

The book that I was reading had colorful pages.

Ⓐ colorful
Ⓑ reading
Ⓒ pages
Ⓓ book

Question 2

Identify the adjective/adjectives in the following sentence.

Earth is the most beautiful planet in the solar system.

Ⓐ Earth
Ⓑ beautiful
Ⓒ system
Ⓓ planet

Question 3

Identify the adjective in this sentence.

The frightened alien ran back into its airship.

Ⓐ airship
Ⓑ alien
Ⓒ frightened
Ⓓ ran

Question 4

Identify the adverb in the following sentence.

The mother was quite unhappy to see her son leave.

Ⓐ quite
Ⓑ unhappy
Ⓒ the
Ⓓ leave

Question 5

Identify the adverb in the following sentence.

The long wait made him utterly tired.

Ⓐ long
Ⓑ wait
Ⓒ tired
Ⓓ utterly

Question 6

Identify the adverb in the following sentence and point out the verb it modifies/ describes.

My clever friend answered all the questions correctly.

Ⓐ adverb: clever ; verb: friend
Ⓑ adverb: correctly ; verb: questions
Ⓒ adverb: correctly ; verb: answered
Ⓓ adverb: clever : verb: question

Question 7

Identify the adverb in the following sentence.

The girl politely asked the boy for her book back.

Ⓐ girl
Ⓑ book
Ⓒ politely
Ⓓ asked

Question 8

Identify the adjective or adjectives in the following sentence.

The polka dot umbrella protected Ted from the cold rain.

- Ⓐ polka dot and protected
- Ⓑ umbrella and polka dot
- Ⓒ umbrella and rain
- Ⓓ polka dot and cold

Question 9

Identify the adverb in the following sentence.

Last night, the whole family slept soundly.

- Ⓐ soundly
- Ⓑ last
- Ⓒ slept
- Ⓓ night

Question 10

Identify the adverb in the following sentence.

The computer printer hardly works.

- Ⓐ computer
- Ⓑ works
- Ⓒ printer
- Ⓓ hardly

Recognize Pronouns (L.6.1.B)

Question 1

Choose the correct pronoun to complete the sentence.

I did it by _____.

Ⓐ me
Ⓑ myself
Ⓒ I
Ⓓ my

Question 2

Choose the correct pronoun to complete the sentence.

We are responsible for the decorations _____.

Ⓐ us
Ⓑ ourselves
Ⓒ themselves
Ⓓ myself

Question 3

Choose the correct pronoun to complete the sentence.

She made up the story _____ .

Ⓐ himself
Ⓑ herself
Ⓒ itself
Ⓓ themself

Question 4

Choose the correct pronoun to complete the sentence.

If a student wants to do well, _____ to get plenty of sleep.

Ⓐ you have
Ⓑ he or she has
Ⓒ you have
Ⓓ they have

Question 5

Choose the correct pronoun to complete the sentence.

The best poker players can keep _____ faces from showing any reaction.

Ⓐ her
Ⓑ its
Ⓒ their
Ⓓ his

Question 6

Correct the following sentence to make the referent clear.

Charlie danced with his friend Carol and Sue most of the evening. She is his girlfriend.

Ⓐ Sue is his girlfriend.
Ⓑ He is her friend.
Ⓒ She is the girlfriend.
Ⓓ Carol is his girlfriend.

Question 7

Correct the following sentence to make the referent clear.

Riding without a helmet is a big risk. This is unnecessary.

Ⓐ They are unnecessary.
Ⓑ This risk is unnecessary.
Ⓒ It is unnecessary.
Ⓓ Riding is unnecessary.

Question 8

Correct the following sentence to make the referent clear.

The cat ate the goldfish before I could stop the tragedy. It was terrible.

Ⓐ They are terrible.
Ⓑ The tragedy was terrible.
Ⓒ The goldfish was terrible.
Ⓓ The cat was terrible.

Question 9

Correct the following sentence to make the referent clear.

Johnny is taller than Ahmed. He's grown a lot this year.

- Ⓐ The boys have grown a lot this year.
- Ⓑ Ahmed has grown a lot this year.
- Ⓒ They have grown a lot this year.
- Ⓓ Johnny has grown a lot this year.

Question 10

Correct the following sentence to make the referent clear.

The Sharks and the Jets were the gangs in West Side Story. They performed great dances.

- Ⓐ The gangs performed great dances.
- Ⓑ The sharks performed great dances.
- Ⓒ It performed great dances.
- Ⓓ The Jets performed great dances.

Recognize and Correct Shifts in Pronoun Number and Person (L.6.1.C)

Question 1

Which pronoun best completes the following sentence?

Each student got to choose _____ own desk.

(A) his
(B) her
(C) their
(D) its

Question 2

Which pronoun best completes the following sentence?

All the girls were excited to be able to wear _____ new dresses to the dance.

(A) the
(B) their
(C) there
(D) her

Question 3

Which pronoun best completes the following sentence?

Coach Bob was proud of the way _____ team played in the game.

(A) their
(B) our
(C) her
(D) his

Question 4

Which pronoun best completes the following sentence?

Billy and _____ plan to ride our bikes to the park as soon as school is out.

- (A) I
- (B) me
- (C) us
- (D) his

Question 5

Which pronoun best completes the following sentence?

Mrs. Marshall's students won the reading contest. _____ read more books than any other class in the sixth grade.

- (A) Their
- (B) Her
- (C) They
- (D) I

Question 6

Which pronoun best completes the following sentence?

Johnny's friends are all on the football team with _____.

- (A) her
- (B) his
- (C) it
- (D) him

Question 7

Which pronoun best completes the following sentence?

Lucy loves pepperoni and onions with extra cheese on _____ pizza.

- (A) her
- (B) their
- (C) his
- (D) my

Question 8

Which pronoun best completes the following sentence?

_____ can't wait to go to see my Aunt Sara for the holidays.

Ⓐ We
Ⓑ He
Ⓒ I
Ⓓ They

Question 9

Which pronoun best completes the following sentence?

When Tiffany went ice skating, _____ fell and twisted her ankle.

Ⓐ she
Ⓑ her
Ⓒ my
Ⓓ we

Question 10

Which pronoun best completes the following sentence?

My dog loves playing catch with his ball, except _____ never brings it back.

Ⓐ they
Ⓑ she
Ⓒ he
Ⓓ I

Recognize and Correct Vague Pronouns (L.6.1.D)

Question 1

Choose the pronoun that agrees with the antecedent in the following sentence.

Anybody who forgets _____ homework will have detention at lunch.

Ⓐ his
Ⓑ my
Ⓒ its
Ⓓ their

Question 2

Choose the pronoun that agrees with the antecedent in the following sentence.

The students made _____ own costumes for the play.

Ⓐ her
Ⓑ their
Ⓒ my
Ⓓ our

Question 3

Choose the pronoun that agrees with the antecedent in the following sentence.

Gavin's dog follows _____ everywhere.

Ⓐ their
Ⓑ me
Ⓒ his
Ⓓ him

Question 4

Choose the pronoun that agrees with the antecedent in the following sentence.

Emily and Nathan both love to sing so _____ are going to do a duet for the talent show

Ⓐ they
Ⓑ he
Ⓒ she
Ⓓ their

Question 5

Choose the pronoun that agrees with the antecedent in the following sentence.

The students practiced many hours in preparation for _____ concert.

(A) their
(B) there
(C) our
(D) his

Question 6

Choose the pronoun that agrees with the antecedent in the following sentence.

Roger stayed up late to finish _____ English project.

(A) our
(B) his
(C) their
(D) my

Question 7

Choose the pronoun that agrees with the antecedent in the following sentence.

Mary left the cookies out on the counter so I ate _____.

(A) it
(B) she
(C) them
(D) their

Question 8

Choose the pronoun that agrees with the antecedent in the following sentence.

The store was having a huge sale on all _____ shoes.

(A) its
(B) her
(C) our
(D) my

Question 9

Choose the pronoun that agrees with the antecedent in the following sentence.

Even though Patty is packed for the trip, _____ does not feel ready to go.

Ⓐ I
Ⓑ she
Ⓒ he
Ⓓ they

Question 10

Choose the pronoun that agrees with the antecedent in the following sentence.

Billy and Luis both forgot to bring _____ sleeping bags on the camping trip.

Ⓐ his
Ⓑ my
Ⓒ our
Ⓓ their

Recognize Variations in English (L.6.1.E)

Question Number 1:

What is the correct way to write the underlined part of the following sentence?

Yesterday my mom baked cookies and we <u>eat</u> them all.

- Ⓐ will eat
- Ⓑ did eat
- Ⓒ eaten
- Ⓓ ate

Question Number 2:

What is the correct way to write the underlined part of the following sentence?

Jenny went to the store and <u>buy</u> apples, milk, and bread.

- Ⓐ bought
- Ⓑ will buy
- Ⓒ did buy
- Ⓓ buyed

Question Number 3:

What is the correct way to write the underlined part of the following sentence?

Billy and Matt rode <u>they're</u> bikes to the park.

- Ⓐ there
- Ⓑ their
- Ⓒ they
- Ⓓ them

Question Number 4:

What is the correct way to write the underlined part of the following sentence?

My dad and I <u>builds</u> a tree house together this weekend.

- Ⓐ will build
- Ⓑ built
- Ⓒ had built
- Ⓓ build

Question Number 5:

What is the correct way to write the underlined part of the following sentence?

They always take such good care of <u>them</u> garden.

- Ⓐ that
- Ⓑ there
- Ⓒ they're
- Ⓓ their

Question Number 6:

What is the correct way to write the underlined part of the sentence?

Tony and Melissa had fun <u>sing</u> in the spring concert.

- Ⓐ sung
- Ⓑ singing
- Ⓒ sang
- Ⓓ will sing

Question Number 7:

What is the correct way to write the underlined part of the sentence?

Debbie always <u>did</u> her homework first thing when she gets home.

- Ⓐ does
- Ⓑ will do
- Ⓒ doesn't do
- Ⓓ didn't

Question Number 8:

What is the correct way to write the underlined part of the sentence?

Mickey's brother always takes <u>him</u> toys.

Ⓐ her
Ⓑ he
Ⓒ their
Ⓓ his

Question Number 9:

What is the correct way to write the underlined part of the sentence?

<u>Them</u> holiday lights are so pretty and sparkly.

Ⓐ They
Ⓑ Her
Ⓒ Those
Ⓓ All

Question Number 10:

What is the correct way to write the underlined part of the sentence?

My dog always runs <u>happy</u> by my side.

Ⓐ with happy
Ⓑ happier
Ⓒ happiest
Ⓓ happily

Demonstrate Command of Punctuation (L.6.2.A)

Question Number 1:

Choose the answer with the correct punctuation for the sentence below.

Hi, Mom I'm home called Robby as he walked through the door

Ⓐ "Hi, Mom! I'm home," called Robby as he walked through the door.
Ⓑ Hi, Mom I'm home called Robby as he walked through the door.
Ⓒ Hi Mom I'm home, called Robby as he walked through the door.
Ⓓ Hi Mom, I'm home, called Robby, as he walked through the door.

Question Number 2:

Choose the answer with the correct punctuation for the sentence below.

I had bananas oranges and cherries in the refrigerator but they're all gone

Ⓐ I had bananas oranges and cherries in the refrigerator but they're all gone.
Ⓑ I had bananas oranges and cherries in the refrigerator, but they're all gone.
Ⓒ I had bananas, oranges, and cherries in the refrigerator, but they're all gone.
Ⓓ I had bananas oranges and cherries, in the refrigerator, but they're all gone.

Question Number 3:

Choose the answer with the correct punctuation for the sentence below.

September is the busiest month of the year that's why it's my favorite

Ⓐ September is the busiest month of the year; that's why it's my favorite.
Ⓑ September is the busiest month of the year that's why it's my favorite.
Ⓒ September, is the busiest month of the year, that's why it's my favorite.
Ⓓ September is the busiest month of the year that's why it's my favorite!

Question Number 4:

Choose the answer with the correct punctuation for the sentence below.

Which one is Olivias jacket the teacher asked

Ⓐ Which one is Olivias jacket the teacher asked?
Ⓑ Which one is Olivia's jacket the teacher asked.
Ⓒ "Which one is Olivia's jacket?" the teacher asked.
Ⓓ Which one is Olivia's jacket the teacher asked!

Question Number 5:

Choose the answer with the correct punctuation for the sentence below.

New Years Day will be on January 1 2012

Ⓐ New Years Day will be on January 1 2012.
Ⓑ New Year's Day will be on January 1, 2012.
Ⓒ New Years Day will be on January, 1, 2012.
Ⓓ New Year's Day, will be on January 1, 2012.

Question Number 6:

Choose the answer with the correct punctuation for the sentence below.

I got into a great college which made my mom happy.

Ⓐ I got in, to a great college which made, my mom happy.
Ⓑ I got in to a great, college which made my mom, happy.
Ⓒ I got into a great college, which made my mom happy.
Ⓓ I got into a great college which, made my mom happy.

Question Number 7:

Choose the answer with the correct punctuation for the sentence below.

Joyce remembered to bring her bathing suit on vacation but she left her sun screen in Dallas Texas.

Ⓐ Joyce remembered to bring her bathing suit on vacation, but she left her sun screen in Dallas, Texas.
Ⓑ Joyce remembered to bring her bathing suit on vacation but she left her sun screen in Dallas, Texas.
Ⓒ Joyce remembered to bring her bathing suit on vacation, but she left her sun screen in Dallas Texas.
Ⓓ Joyce remembered to bring her bathing suit, on vacation, but she left her sun screen, in Dallas, Texas.

Question Number 8:

Choose the answer with the correct punctuation for the sentence below.

Have you ever been to Albany New York, or Flourtown Pennsylvania.

Ⓐ Have you ever been to Albany, New York, or Flourtown Pennsylvania?
Ⓑ Have you ever been to Albany, New York or Flourtown, Pennsylvania.
Ⓒ Have you ever been to Albany New York, or Flourtown, Pennsylvania.
Ⓓ Have you ever been to Albany, New York or Flourtown, Pennsylvania?

Question Number 9:

Choose the answer with the correct punctuation for the sentence below.

Ryan stated "you shouldnt bully other kids.

Ⓐ Ryan stated, you shouldn't bully other kids.
Ⓑ Ryan stated, "you shouldnt bully other kids"
Ⓒ Ryan stated, "you shouldnt bully other kids.
Ⓓ Ryan stated, "You shouldn't bully other kids."

Question Number 10:

Choose the answer with the correct punctuation for the sentence below.

Michelle made pizza grilled cheese and tacos for lunch but she didnt realize it was only 10:00 a.m.

Ⓐ Michelle made pizza, grilled, cheese, and tacos for lunch but she didnt realize that it was only 10:00 a.m.
Ⓑ Michelle made pizza, grilled cheese, and tacos for lunch, but she didnt realize, it was only 10:00 a.m.
Ⓒ Michelle made pizza, grilled cheese, and tacos for lunch, but she didn't realize that it was only 10:00 a.m.
Ⓓ Michelle made pizza, grilled, cheese, and tacos for lunch, but she didn't realize, it was only 10:00 am.

Correct Spelling (L.6.2.B)

Question Number 1:

Choose the correct word that fits the blank:

Grind the wheat to a powdery _____.

Ⓐ flower
Ⓑ flour
Ⓒ floor
Ⓓ floure

Question Number 2:

Choose the correct word that fits the blank:

Among all _____, my favorite is the pink rose.

Ⓐ floors
Ⓑ flour
Ⓒ flowers
Ⓓ floures

Question Number 3:

Choose the correct word that fits the blank:

The last _____ creaked as I stepped on to it.

Ⓐ stare
Ⓑ stair
Ⓒ steer
Ⓓ stiar

Question Number 4:

Choose the correct word that fits in the blank:

He _____ the ball and it flew forward.

Ⓐ through
Ⓑ threw
Ⓒ throw
Ⓓ any of the above

Question Number 5:

Choose the answer with the correct set of words, in the given order, to fill in the blanks in the sentence below.

I am _____ fed up by all the noise in the city, and hence am heading to the countryside for some peace and _____ .

Ⓐ quiet, quite
Ⓑ quite, quiet
Ⓒ quite, quite
Ⓓ quiet, quiet

Question Number 6:

Choose the correct word to fill in the blank in the sentence below.

Britney _____ a car for her 18th birthday.

Ⓐ received
Ⓑ recieved
Ⓒ purschesed
Ⓓ baught

Question Number 7:

Choose the correct word to fill in the blank in the sentence below.

The boy was very _____ about King Tut and Egypt.

Ⓐ nowledgeable
Ⓑ knowlegeable
Ⓒ knowledgeable
Ⓓ knoledgable

Question Number 8:

Choose the correct word to fill in the blank in the sentence below.

The black and white cat had really long _____ .

Ⓐ whiskers
Ⓑ whisckers
Ⓒ wisikers
Ⓓ None of the above

Question Number 9:

Choose the correct word to fill in the blank in the sentence below.

My favorite_____ is a small Italian place on Elm Street.

Ⓐ restrant
Ⓑ resturannt
Ⓒ restaurant
Ⓓ restraent

Question Number 10:

Choose the correct word to fill in the blank in the sentence below.

The _____ of the school gave a student detention.

Ⓐ Principle
Ⓑ Princapal
Ⓒ Principel
Ⓓ Principal

Knowledge of Language

Vary Sentence (L.6.3.A)

Question Number 1:

What is the best way to combine the following sentences?

The oven temperature was too hot. The cookies got burnt.

Ⓐ   The oven temperature was too hot, the cookies got burnt.
Ⓑ   The oven temperature was too hot because the cookies got burnt.
Ⓒ   The oven temperature was too hot the cookies got burnt.
Ⓓ   The oven temperature was too hot, so the cookies got burnt.

Question Number 2:

What is the best way to combine the following sentences?

Mike and Johnny wanted to play outside. It was raining so they couldn't.

Ⓐ   Mike and Johnny wanted to play outside, but it was raining.
Ⓑ   Because of the rain, Mike and Johnny couldn't play outside.
Ⓒ   Mike and Johnny wanted to play outside and it was raining so they couldn't.
Ⓓ   Mike and Johnny wanted to play outside in the rain.

Question Number 3:

What is the best way to combine the following sentences?

I would like to have pizza at my party. I would also like to have ice cream and chocolate cake.

Ⓐ   I would like to have pizza at my party, and I would also like to have ice cream and chocolate cake.
Ⓑ   I would like to have pizza at my party, and ice cream and chocolate cake.
Ⓒ   I would like to have pizza, ice cream, and chocolate cake at my party.
Ⓓ   At my party, I would like to have pizza and ice cream and chocolate cake.

Question Number 4:

What is the best way to combine the following sentences?

We should go to the mall. After school.

Ⓐ   After school, we should go to the mall.
Ⓑ   We should go to the mall, after school.
Ⓒ   We should go to the mall, and after school.
Ⓓ   After school, to the mall we should go.

Question Number 5:

Which is the best way to combine the following sentences?

The cat chases the dog. The dog chases the cat.

Ⓐ   The cat chases the dog, and the dog chases the cat.
Ⓑ   The cat chases the dog, but the dog chases the cat.
Ⓒ   The cat chases the dog, the dog chases the cat.
Ⓓ   The cat and dog chase each other.

Question Number 6:

Which is the best way to combine the following sentences?

Summer is nice. Spring is my favorite.

Ⓐ   Summer is nice, and spring is my favorite.
Ⓑ   Summer is nice, spring is my favorite.
Ⓒ   Summer is nice, but spring is my favorite.
Ⓓ   Summer and spring are nice.

Question Number 7:

Which is the best way to combine the following sentences?

We will be going camping. After school on Friday.

Ⓐ   We will be going camping, and after school on Friday.
Ⓑ   After school on Friday, we will be going camping.
Ⓒ   After school on Friday we will be going camping.
Ⓓ   Camping we are going after school on Friday.

Question Number 8:

Which is the best way to combine the following sentences?

Before the party I have to wash the dishes. I also have to do the laundry. And walk the dog.

Ⓐ Before the party I have to wash the dishes. I also have to do the laundry and walk the dog.
Ⓑ Before the party I have to wash the dishes do the laundry and walk the dog.
Ⓒ Before the party, I have to wash the dishes, do the laundry and walk the dog.
Ⓓ I have to wash the dishes. I also have to do the laundry and walk the dog. Before the party.

Question Number 9:

Which is the best way to combine the following sentences?

Lisa got a book. She got it at the library.

Ⓐ Lisa got a book at the library.
Ⓑ Lisa got a book, and she got it at the library.
Ⓒ Lisa got a book, so she got it at the library.
Ⓓ At the library, Lisa got her book.

Question Number 10:

Which is the best way to combine the following sentences?

The puppy was soft and cuddly. It was brown.

Ⓐ The puppy was soft and cuddly, and it was brown.
Ⓑ The brown puppy was soft and cuddly.
Ⓒ The puppy was soft and cuddly and brown.
Ⓓ The puppy was brown and it was soft and it was cuddly.

Maintain Consistency in Style and Tone (L.6.3.B)

Question Number 1:

Which of the following sentences paints the clearest picture?

Ⓐ Even though the sun was shining, Mary couldn't help but feel chilled by the cool morning breeze.
Ⓑ Even though the sun was shining, Mary was still cold.
Ⓒ The sun was shining but the breeze made Mary cold.
Ⓓ Mary was chilled on the sunny, yet breeze morning.

Question Number 2:

Which of the following sentences uses the most descriptive words and style?

Ⓐ As the darkness fell, Scott was scared of what might be out there.
Ⓑ As the darkness fell, Scott couldn't help but be weary of what might lurk out there in the shadows.
Ⓒ As the darkness fell, Scott was frightened by what he could not see.
Ⓓ Scott is scared of the dark.

Question Number 3:

Which of the following sentences provides the most detail about the topic?

Ⓐ Callie loved the smell of cookies.
Ⓑ Callie loved the smell of her mother's cookies.
Ⓒ Callie loved the smell of her mother's fresh baked cookies.
Ⓓ Callie loved the smell of her mother's fresh baked chocolate chip cookies.

Question Number 4:

Which of the following sentences provides sufficient information in an efficient format?

Ⓐ George Washington was the first president. He was also a general in the American Revolution.
Ⓑ George Washington was not only the first president, but he was also a general in the American Revolution.
Ⓒ George Washington was a general and president.
Ⓓ George Washington was the first president and a general in the American Revolution.

Question Number 5:

Which of the following sentences is most concise?

Ⓐ I loved the movie. I just didn't like the surprise ending.
Ⓑ I loved the movie, and I just didn't like the surprise ending.
Ⓒ I loved the movie, but I just didn't like the surprise ending.
Ⓓ I loved the movie, but I didn't like the surprise ending.

Question Number 6:

Which of the following sentences is the most concise and accurate?

Ⓐ I'm so nervous for the play. What if I forget my lines? What if I fall down and everyone laughs at me?
Ⓑ I'm so nervous for the play. What if I forget my lines, fall down, and everyone laughs at me?
Ⓒ I'm so nervous for the play. What if I forget my lines or fall down and everyone laughs at me?
Ⓓ I am nervous that I will forget my lines. I am nervous I will fall down and everyone will laugh at me.

Question Number 7:

Which of the following sentences provides the most imaginative style?

Ⓐ After the dog got out of the yard, Freddie ran after it.
Ⓑ The dog got out of the yard. Freddie ran after it.
Ⓒ Freddie ran after the dog, after it got out of the yard.
Ⓓ The dog got out of the yard and Freddie ran after it.

Question Number 8:

Which of the following sentences provides the most detailed concise expression of the events?

Ⓐ Seth and Iris walked on the beach. They collected sea shells.
Ⓑ As they walked along the beach, Seth and Iris collected sea shells.
Ⓒ Seth and Iris walked and collected sea shells.
Ⓓ At the beach, Seth and Iris walked. They also collected sea shells.

Question Number 9:

Which of the following sentences is the most concise?

Ⓐ Beth thought the test was hard and difficult. Mary thought the test was easy.
Ⓑ While Beth thought the test was challenging, Mary thought it was easy.
Ⓒ Beth thought the test was hard and Mary thought it was easy.
Ⓓ Beth thought the test was hard and difficult, but Mary thought the test was easy.

Question Number 10:

Which of the following sentences uses the smoothest and most concise language to describe the event?

Ⓐ The lights slowly darkened to signal the start of the movie. Mark and Anthony got excited.
Ⓑ The lights slowly darkened to signal the start of the movie, and Mark and Anthony got excited.
Ⓒ Mark and Anthony got excited when the lights slowly darkened to signal the start of the movie.
Ⓓ The lights went out so the movie could start. Mark and Anthony got excited.

Vocabulary Acquisition and Use

Use Context Clues to Determine Word Meaning (L.6.4.A)

Question Number 1:

Julio was happy and astounded when he won MVP for the soccer season. He had been sure that Reuben or Carlos were going to be chosen.

The word "astounded" in this context means: _____.

Ⓐ disappointed
Ⓑ very surprised
Ⓒ satisfied
Ⓓ pleased

Question Number 2:

A spider web may look flimsy, but spider silk is actually five times stronger than steel. It is tougher, stronger, and more flexible than anything humans have been able to produce.

The word "flimsy" in this context means: _____.

Ⓐ beautiful
Ⓑ silky
Ⓒ weak
Ⓓ inflexible

Question Number 3:

New Jersey is on the east coast of the Mid-Atlantic region of the United States of America. It is bordered by the Atlantic Ocean to the east and by Delaware to the southwest, Pennsylvania to the west, and New York to the north and northeast. Parts of the state are suburbs of New York City, just across the Hudson River to the northeast, and Philadelphia, just across the Delaware River on the southwest.

In the above context, "bordered" means _____.

Ⓐ surrounded by
Ⓑ marked by
Ⓒ differentiated by
Ⓓ separated by

Question Number 4:

Africa is a very diverse continent, with each country, or even each part of a country, having its own unique culture. While it is common for people in the West to refer to Africa as if it was a single country, one should remember the sheer size of the continent. Africa is not one country but 55 different countries, meaning that it is impossible to make generalizations about Africa as a whole.

In the above context, "sheer" means _____.

Ⓐ vast
Ⓑ transparent
Ⓒ unmixed
Ⓓ small

Question Number 5:

My dog is devoted to my family. He would never leave us.

In the above context, "devoted" means _____

Ⓐ loyal
Ⓑ loving
Ⓒ unloving
Ⓓ hated

Question Number 6:

It is always beneficial to eat your vegetables. That's why your doctor tells you to eat plenty of fruits and vegetables.

In the above context, "beneficial" means _____

Ⓐ horrible
Ⓑ wrong
Ⓒ good for you
Ⓓ nice

Question Number 7:

The stench coming from the garbage can was unbearable.

In the above context, "stench" means _____

(A) sugary
(B) freshness
(C) sweetness
(D) stink

Question Number 8:

The celebrity walked the red carpet and was overwhelmed by the barrage of questions from reporters.

In the above context, "barrage" means _____

(A) abundance
(B) few
(C) twenty
(D) little

Question Number 9:

The sweltering summer heat made the beach unpleasant.

In the above context, "sweltering" means _____

(A) cold
(B) frigid
(C) hot
(D) humid

Question Number 10:

The big, nasty creature was brown and hairy; it looked hideous.

In the above context, "hideous" means _____

(A) ugly
(B) pretty
(C) sad
(D) beautiful

Use Common Roots and Affixes (L.6.4.B)

Question Number 1:

Which of the following is a true statement?

Ⓐ A suffix or ending is an affix, which is placed at the end of a word.
Ⓑ A prefix or beginning is an affix, which is placed at the beginning of a word.
Ⓒ A suffix is attached at the beginning of the word.
Ⓓ Both A and B

Question Number 2:

When the suffix "-able" is added to the word "cap", it means-

Ⓐ able to do something
Ⓑ to do anything
Ⓒ not able to do something
Ⓓ not able to do anything

Question Number 3:

Identify the suffix in the following words:

Salvage, Storage, Forage

Ⓐ A
Ⓑ ge
Ⓒ age
Ⓓ rage

Question Number 4:

Identify the prefix in the following words.

Anarchy, Anonymous, Anemia

Ⓐ Anna
Ⓑ An
Ⓒ Ana
Ⓓ Both A and B

Question Number 5:

What does the suffix "less" mean?

- Ⓐ Too little
- Ⓑ With
- Ⓒ Without
- Ⓓ None of the above

Question Number 6:

What does the suffix "ology" mean?

- Ⓐ Study
- Ⓑ Vocabulary
- Ⓒ Sadness
- Ⓓ Study of animals

Question Number 7:

Identify the meaning of the root word in the in the following words:

Commemorate, Commune, Community

- Ⓐ Far apart
- Ⓑ Uncommon
- Ⓒ Together
- Ⓓ Unlikely

Question Number 8:

Which of the following statements is true?

- Ⓐ The first rule of decoding words is to find out if the word has any suffixes or prefixes
- Ⓑ You should always divide between the consonants
- Ⓒ Both A and B
- Ⓓ None of the above

Question Number 9:

Using the rule 'divide between the consonants', decode the word 'sentence'.

- Ⓐ se-n-tence
- Ⓑ sen-tence
- Ⓒ sen-ten-ce
- Ⓓ none of the above

Question Number 10:

What is the correct way to decode the word 'Monarch'

Ⓐ mona-rch
Ⓑ mon-ar-ch
Ⓒ mon-a-rch
Ⓓ mon-arch

Consult Reference Materials (L.6.4.C)

Question Number 1:

Alphabetize the following words:

hibiscus, petunia, rose, honeysuckle, daffodil

Ⓐ hibiscus, petunia, rose, honeysuckle, daffodil
Ⓑ daffodil, hibiscus, honeysuckle, petunia, rose
Ⓒ daffodil, honeysuckle, hibiscus, petunia, rose
Ⓓ hibiscus, petunia, rose, daffodil, honeysuckle

Question Number 2:

Alphabetize the following words:

mouse, mule, monkey, moose, mole

Ⓐ mouse, monkey, moose, mole, mule
Ⓑ mouse, mule, monkey, moose, mole
Ⓒ mouse, moose, monkey, mole, mule
Ⓓ mole, monkey, moose, mouse, mule

Question Number 3:

Alphabetize the following words:

sustain, solicit, sizzle, sanitize, secure

Ⓐ sustain, solicit, sizzle, sanitize, secure
Ⓑ sanitize, secure, sustain, solicit, sizzle
Ⓒ sanitize, solicit, sizzle, sustain, sizzle,
Ⓓ sanitize, secure, sizzle, solicit, sustain

Question Number 4:

The dictionary contains _____.

Ⓐ meaning of a word
Ⓑ pronunciation of a word
Ⓒ the etymology (where the word came from)
Ⓓ all the above

Question Number 5:

Which of the following answer choices can you find in a thesaurus?

(A) homonym
(B) homograph
(C) synonym
(D) definition

Question Number 6:

How do you go about starting to find a word you are looking for in the dictionary?

(A) Open the dictionary
(B) Open the dictionary to the page that has the first two letters of the word you are looking for
(C) Open the dictionary to the page that has the last two letters of the word
(D) Open the dictionary and look in the table of contents

Question Number 7:

What are guidewords in a dictionary?

(A) Guidewords are words that tell you how to pronounce your word
(B) Guidewords are located at the bottom of each page
(C) Guidewords are words that tell you the part of speech of your word
(D) Guidewords are at the top of each page to tell you the first and last words you will find on that page.

Question Number 8:

How many syllables are in the word "organized?"

(A) 3
(B) 4
(C) 6
(D) 1

Question Number 9:

How many syllables are in the word "jacket?"

Ⓐ 1
Ⓑ 3
Ⓒ 2
Ⓓ 4

Question Number 10:

How many syllables would you have, if you divide the word 'hyacinth'?

Ⓐ 2
Ⓑ 3
Ⓒ 8
Ⓓ 4

Determine the Meaning of a Word (L.6.4.D)

Question Number 1:

What does the underlined word in the sentence mean?

Johnny was certain he hadn't <u>misplaced</u> his glove but he couldn't find it.

Ⓐ found
Ⓑ lost
Ⓒ hid
Ⓓ borrowed

Question Number 2:

What does the underlined word in the sentence mean?

Despite the <u>brisk</u> temperatures, football fans still packed the stadium to watch the championship game.

Ⓐ hot
Ⓑ fast
Ⓒ cool
Ⓓ exciting

Question Number 3:

What does the underlined word in the sentence mean?

Natalie and Sophia couldn't wait to ride the roller coaster. They'd heard it was very <u>exhilarating</u>.

Ⓐ fast
Ⓑ frightening
Ⓒ exciting
Ⓓ boring

Question Number 4:

What does the underlined word in the sentence mean?

Billy always found raking leaves to be a very <u>mundane</u> chore. It was the same thing over and over.

Ⓐ fun
Ⓑ challenging
Ⓒ easy
Ⓓ boring

Question Number 5:

What does the underlined word in the sentence mean?

The whimpering puppies were clearly <u>ravenous</u>. They devoured the food when it was ready.

- Ⓐ hungry
- Ⓑ sleepy
- Ⓒ playful
- Ⓓ scared

Question Number 6:

What does the underlined word in the sentence mean?

The basketball team had <u>triumphed</u> over their opponents.

- Ⓐ lost
- Ⓑ forfeited
- Ⓒ competed
- Ⓓ won

Question Number 7:

What does the underlined word in the sentence mean?

Abby found the new student to be <u>bewitching</u>.

- Ⓐ scary
- Ⓑ charming
- Ⓒ kind
- Ⓓ boring

Question Number 8:

What does the underlined word in the sentence mean?

Julia found fishing to be completely <u>repulsing</u>. She wanted nothing to do with putting the worm on the hook.

- Ⓐ wonderful
- Ⓑ delightful
- Ⓒ relaxing
- Ⓓ awful

Question Number 9:

What does the underlined word in the sentence mean?

As Tony and Steve climbed higher and higher up the mountainside, they noticed everything took on a whole new <u>perspective</u>.

Ⓐ appearance
Ⓑ experience
Ⓒ height
Ⓓ altitude

Question Number 10:

If you do not know what a word means, where can you look?

Ⓐ Dictionary
Ⓑ Thesaurus
Ⓒ Glossary
Ⓓ All of the above

Interpret Figures of Speech (L.6.5.A)

Question Number 1:

What type(s) of figurative language is(are) being used in the sentence below?

Jimmy and Johnny jumped like jelly beans.

- (A) Metaphor
- (B) Idiom
- (C) Personification
- (D) Alliteration

Question Number 2:

What type of figurative language is being used in the sentence below?

Don't spill the beans.

- (A) Idiom
- (B) Onomatopoeia
- (C) Personification
- (D) Alliteration

Question Number 3:

What type of figurative language is being used in the sentence below?

That sandwich is as big as a car.

- (A) Personification
- (B) Simile
- (C) Metaphor
- (D) Alliteration

Question Number 4:

What type of figurative language is being used in the sentence below?

We better cook a lot of food; we have an army to feed.

- (A) Hyperbole
- (B) Alliteration
- (C) Idiom
- (D) Personification

Question Number 5:

What type of figurative language is being used in the sentence below?

The baby bear looked up at its mother with adoring eyes filled with love.

- Ⓐ Idiom
- Ⓑ Alliteration
- Ⓒ Personification
- Ⓓ Metaphor

Question Number 6:

What type of figurative language is being used in the sentence below?

Zoom, roared the car engine.

- Ⓐ Personification
- Ⓑ Simile
- Ⓒ Idiom
- Ⓓ Onomatopoeia

Question Number 7:

What type of figurative language is being used in the sentence below?

Katy is a pig when she eats.

- Ⓐ Simile
- Ⓑ Metaphor
- Ⓒ Onomatopoeia
- Ⓓ Alliteration

Question Number 8:

What type of figurative language is being used in the sentence below?

Yesterday was the worst day of my entire life.

- Ⓐ Alliteration
- Ⓑ Hyperbole
- Ⓒ Idiom
- Ⓓ Simile

Question Number 9:

What type of figurative language is being used in the sentence below?

Stop pulling my leg..

Ⓐ Idiom
Ⓑ Alliteration
Ⓒ Personification
Ⓓ Onomatopoeia

Question Number 10:

What type of figurative language is being used in the sentence below?

Danielle's dancing is as graceful as a swan.

Ⓐ Metaphor
Ⓑ Simile
Ⓒ Personification
Ⓓ Hyperbole

Use Relationships to Better Understand Words (L.6.5.B)

Question Number 1:

Identify the cause and the effect in the following sentence:

The blizzard was so widespread that all flights were cancelled.

cause _____ effect _____

- Ⓐ cause-blizzard; effect- flights cancelled
- Ⓑ cause-flights; effect- blizzard
- Ⓒ cause-blizzard; effect- flights
- Ⓓ cause-cancelled flights; effect- widespread blizzard

Question Number 2:

Identify the cause and the effect in the following sentence:

Several hundred people were left homeless by the flood.

cause _____ effect _____

- Ⓐ cause- homeless people; effect -flood
- Ⓑ cause- flood; effect - people left homeless
- Ⓒ cause- people; effect -homeless
- Ⓓ cause- flood; effect -several hundred people

Question Number 3:

Identify the cause and the effect in the following sentence:

Pedro's friendly attitude got him the job.

cause _____ effect _____

- Ⓐ cause- Pedro; effect- friendly attitude
- Ⓑ cause- Pedro; effect- got the job
- Ⓒ cause- friendly attitude; effect- got the job
- Ⓓ cause- job; effect- friendly attitude

Question Number 4:

Match the following item with the category to which it belongs:
mammals: _____

Ⓐ giraffe
Ⓑ cheese
Ⓒ frogs
Ⓓ bees

Question Number 5:

Match the following item with the category to which it belongs:

birds: _____

Ⓐ parrots
Ⓑ giraffes
Ⓒ bees
Ⓓ sharks

Question Number 6:

Match the following item with the category to which it belongs:

desserts: _____

Ⓐ elephants
Ⓑ pie
Ⓒ carrots
Ⓓ cheese

Question Number 7:

**This exercise will help you practice identifying parts and wholes.
Arrange the following words in order by size:**

galaxy, universe, county, country, town, neighborhood, state, world, continent, solar system
hemisphere.

A street is part of a _____,
which is part of a _____,
which is part of a _____,
which is part of a _____,
which is part of a _____,
which is part of a _____,
which is part of a _____,
which is part of a _____,
which is part of a _____,
which is part of a _____,
which is part of a _____,
which is part of a _____.

Ⓐ town; neighborhood; county; state; country; continent; galaxy; hemisphere; world; universe; solar system

Ⓑ world; solar system; galaxy; universe; neighborhood; town; county; state; country; continent; hemisphere;

Ⓒ neighborhood; town; county; state; country; continent; hemisphere; world; solar system; galaxy; universe

Ⓓ neighborhood; galaxy; universe; town; county; state; country; hemisphere; world; solar system; continent

Question Number 8:

Match the following item with the category to which it belongs:

insects: _____

Ⓐ sharks
Ⓑ bees
Ⓒ frogs
Ⓓ parrots

Question Number 9:

Identify the cause and the effect in the following sentence:

The burned popcorn made the whole house smell like smoke.

cause _____ effect _____

Ⓐ cause-popcorn; effect- smoke
Ⓑ cause- burned popcorn; effect- smoky smell
Ⓒ cause-house; effect- burned popcorn
Ⓓ cause-smoky smell; effect- burned popcorn

Question Number 10:

Identify the cause and the effect in the following sentence:

He practiced until he could make 3 out of 4 free throws.

cause _____ effect _____

Ⓐ cause- free throws; effect-practice
Ⓑ cause- practice; effect- four free throws
Ⓒ cause- practice; effect- make three out of four free throws
Ⓓ cause- free throws; effect- three throws

Distinguish Between Word Associations and Definitions (L.6.5.C)

Question Number 1:

Denotation of a word is the _____.

Ⓐ slang for a word.
Ⓑ literal meaning.
Ⓒ part of speech of a word.
Ⓓ feelings we have about a word.

Question Number 2:

Connotation refers to _____.

Ⓐ the literal meaning of a word.
Ⓑ the part of speech of a word.
Ⓒ how we feel about a word.
Ⓓ the slang meaning of a word.

Question Number 3:

Which of the following words has the same denotative meaning as the word house?

Ⓐ dwelling
Ⓑ abode
Ⓒ residence
Ⓓ All of the above

Question Number 4:

Which of the following words has the same denotative meaning as the word child.

Ⓐ elderly
Ⓑ ancient
Ⓒ adolescent
Ⓓ None of the above

Question Number 5:

Which of the following words have the same denotation?

Ⓐ smelly; smiley
Ⓑ sweet; sweat
Ⓒ trash; garbage
Ⓓ stubborn; easy-going

Question Number 6:

Which of the following words have the same denotation?

Ⓐ expensive; cheap
Ⓑ short; tall
Ⓒ rabbit; horse
Ⓓ curious; nosy

Question Number 7:

The word "inexpensive" has a positive connotation.

Which of the following words has the same denotation but a negative connotation?

Ⓐ costly
Ⓑ expensive
Ⓒ free
Ⓓ cheap

Question Number 8:

The word "disaster" has a negative connotation.

Which of the following words has the same denotation but a positive connotation?

Ⓐ Catastrophe
Ⓑ Calamity
Ⓒ Emergency
Ⓓ Tragedy

Question Number 9:

The word "messy" has a positive connotation.

Which of the following words has the same denotation but a negative connotation?

Ⓐ Filthy
Ⓑ Disorganized
Ⓒ Muddled
Ⓓ Sloppy

Question Number 10:

The word "old" has a negative connotation.

Which of the following words has the same denotation but a positive connotation?

Ⓐ Decrepit
Ⓑ Ancient
Ⓒ Elderly
Ⓓ Over the hill

Name: _____ Date: _____

Use Grade Appropriate Words (L.6.6)

Question Number 1:

The word "racket" has multiple meanings.

Which sentence uses the word "racket" where it means "noise?"

(A) I nearly forgot my racket before tennis practice.
(B) There was a lot of racket coming from my brother's room.
(C) My racket broke when I dropped it down the stairs.
(D) I hope I get a new racket for my birthday.

Question Number 2:

The word "bear" has multiple meanings.

Which sentence uses the word "bear" where it means "to hold up?"

(A) The baby bear is so cute!
(B) I cannot bear to see someone hurt.
(C) That apple tree sure does bear a lot of fruit.
(D) I can't bear to stand on my broken ankle.

Question Number 3:

The word "patient" has multiple meanings.

Which sentence uses the word "patient" where it means "quietly waiting?"

(A) The doctor sent the patient for x-rays of her wrist.
(B) The nurse checked on the patient frequently.
(C) The little boy is being very patient in line.
(D) The patient needs to go home and rest before he feels better.

Question Number 4:

The word "pound" has multiple meanings.

Which sentence uses the word "pound" where it means "to hit?"

(A) We got our new dog from the pound.
(B) Jimmy had to pound on the box to get it to break open.
(C) The watermelon weighs 16 pounds!
(D) Sixteen ounces is equal to one pound.

Question Number 5:

The word "pack" has multiple meanings.

Which sentence uses the word "pack" where it means "a group of animals?"

Ⓐ Did you see that pack of wolves down in the valley?
Ⓑ Don't forget to pack your toothbrush.
Ⓒ I packed a sandwich, an apple, and a cookie in your lunch.
Ⓓ Marissa put her pack on her back.

Question Number 6:

Which of the following words best complete the sentence?

Even though I studied, I feel very _____ about the test in Science.

Ⓐ excited
Ⓑ anxious
Ⓒ happy
Ⓓ ready

Question Number 7:

Which of the following words best completes the sentence?

I can't believe how _____ the Grand Canyon is.

Ⓐ immense
Ⓑ small
Ⓒ brown
Ⓓ stationary

Question Number 8:

Which of the following words best completes the sentence?

They say the race is very _____ , so I had better spend some extra time training.

Ⓐ easy
Ⓑ smooth
Ⓒ distinct
Ⓓ rigorous

Question Number 9:

Which of the following words best completes the sentence?

Joey got himself into quite a _____ when he cheated on the test.

Ⓐ predicament
Ⓑ problem
Ⓒ challenge
Ⓓ bit of luck

Question Number 10:

Which of the following words best completes the sentence?

The team was very _____ about practicing.

Ⓐ lazy
Ⓑ sloppy
Ⓒ successful
Ⓓ diligent

End of Language

Answer Key and Detailed Explanations

Language

Correct Use of Adjectives and Adverbs (L.6.1.A)

Question No.	Answer	Detailed Explanations
1	A	The answer is A, colorful. Adjectives are words that describe nouns, and colorful describes the pages. Reading is a verb (with the helping verb was.) Pages and book are both nouns because they are things.
2	B	The answer is B. Adjectives are words that describe nouns, and beautiful describes the noun planet. Earth is a proper noun and both system and plant are nouns.
3	C	The correct answer is C. Alien and airship are both nouns and ran is a verb. Frightened is the only describing word.
4	A	The answer is A. Adverbs answer the questions **how, how often, when, where, how much, or to what extent**. "Quite" shows to what extent the mother was unhappy.
5	D	The answer is D. Adverbs answer the questions **how, how often, when, where, how much, or to what extent**. Utterly shows to what extent the man was tired.
6	C	The answer is C. Once you find the verb (which is answered), ask yourself, "How were all of the questions answered?" "They were answered correctly." That's how you find the adverb.
7	C	Adverbs answer the questions **how, how often, when, where, how much, or to what extent**. The correct answer is C, "politely." This tells us **how** the girl asked for her book.
8	D	The answer is D. "Polka dot" and "cold" are both adjectives (or describing words) that describe the nouns "umbrella" and "rain." Protected is a verb, so these are the only two choices for adjectives.
9	A	Adverbs answer the questions **how, how often, when, where, how much, or to what extent**. The answer is A, "soundly." This modifies the verb "slept" and tells us HOW the family slept.
10	D	Adverbs answer the questions **how, how often, when, where, how much, or to what extent**. The answer is D, "hardly." This tells us **to what extent** the printer works.

Recognize Pronouns (L.6.1.B)

Question No.	Answer	Detailed Explanations
1	B	Answer choice B is correct. "Myself" is a reflexive pronoun. None of the other answer choices sound correct.
2	B	The correct answer is B, "ourselves", because "we" is the subject. That tells us that it is more than one person and the author is included in the decorating.
3	B	Because "she" is used in the sentence, we know the answer is B "herself". The other three answers do not make sense in the sentence.
4	B	The correct answer is B. "A student" is the referent of the pronoun in the sentence. That's how we know to use "he or she has" in the blank. "You" does not make sense because its 2nd person, and "a student" is 3rd person. For that reason, it can't be A or C. "They" is 3rd person, but is referring to more than one person.
5	C	The correct answer is C. The referent of the pronoun is "players", so we know the pronoun should be plural. "Her", "its", and "his" are all singular pronouns.
6	A	They mention that Carol is his friend, so we know that Sue is his girlfriend. The answer is A.
7	B	It mentions that riding without a helmet is a risk. We know from that, what the risk is. The answer is B.
8	B	The tragedy mentioned (the cat eating the goldfish) is what was terrible, so the answer is B.
9	D	Since it says Johnny is taller than Ahmed, then we know they are talking about how much Johnny has grown. The correct answer is D.
10	A	The Sharks and Jets performed great dances, so they is appropriate. The answer is A.

Recognize and Correct Shifts in Pronoun Number and Person (L.6.1.C)

Question No.	Answer	Detailed Explanations
1	C	Since we don't know whether the students are boys or girls, choices A and B will not work. Choice D just does not make sense. Answer choice C is correct because not only does it make sense but it is also gender neutral.
2	B	While we know that her is a pronoun for girl, D is still not the correct answer choice because the sentence references girls (plural) and her is a singular pronoun. "The" does not fit in the sentence. "There" is the incorrect homophone choice. Answer choice B is the correct answer.
3	D	Since we know that Coach Bob is a boy and is singular, the correct answer would be D, "his."
4	A	The only answer choice that is grammatically correct is A, I. "Billy and me," does not sound right, nor does "Billy and us" or "Billy and his."
5	C	Since the sentence is talking about Mrs. Marshall's students, which is a collective grouping of students, we need to look for an answer choice which is plural. The best answer choice is C, "they."
6	D	Since Johnny is a boy, we need to find an answer which reflects this. The best choice is answer D, "him."
7	A	Since Lucy is a girl, we know we are looking for a pronoun that represents a girl. The correct answer is A, "her."
8	C	When talking about Aunt Sara, the sentence says "my" which means one. Therefore, answer choices A and D will not work because they are both plurals. "He" isn't quite right because we don't know who he is. The correct answer choice is C, "I."
9	A	Since Tiffany is a girl, we are looking for an answer that supports this. "Her" doesn't sound right, so "she," answer A, is the correct answer.
10	C	The sentence talks about one dog who likes playing catch with his ball, therefore we are looking for a pronoun that is singular and male. The correct answer is C, "he."

Recognize and Correct Vague Pronouns (L.6.1.D)

Question No.	Answer	Detailed Explanations
1	D	The antecedent in the sentence is anybody, therefore the correct pronoun would be their. No other pronouns make sense. The correct answer is D.
2	B	The antecedent in the sentence is students, therefore the correct pronoun would be their. No other pronoun makes sense. The correct answer is B
3	D	The antecedent in the sentence is Gavin, which is a single boy, therefore the correct pronoun would be him. The correct answer is D.
4	A	The antecedents in the sentence are Emily and Nathan. Since there are two of them, the correct pronoun needs to be plural. The correct answer is A, they.
5	A	The antecedent in the sentence is students, therefore the correct pronoun would be their. There would not be correct because it is not the correct use of the word. No other pronouns make sense. The correct answer is A.
6	B	The antecedent in the sentence is Roger. Since Roger is a single boy, the correct pronoun would be B, his.
7	C	The antecedent in the sentence is cookies. The only pronoun which makes sense is them. The correct answer is C.
8	A	The antecedent in the sentence is store. The correct pronoun would be its. No other pronoun makes sense. The correct answer is A.
9	B	The antecedent in the sentence is Patty. Since Patty is a singular girl, the correct pronoun is she. The correct answer is B.
10	D	The antecedents in the story are Billy and Luis. Since there are two of them, the pronoun should represent two individuals not one. The only pronoun that correctly completes the sentence is D, their.

Recognize Variations in English (L.6.1.E)

Question No.	Answer	Detailed Explanations
1	D	The sentence says that mom made cookies yesterday which means it happened in the past. Therefore, you need to find an answer that is written in the past tense. Answer choice B is future. Answer choices A, C, and D are all past but only D makes sense. The correct answer is D.
2	A	The word "went" tells us this sentence is written in past tense. The only answer that is in past tense and makes sense is A, "bought."
3	B	While they're sounds right, the correct word would actually be their as it shows possession. They're represents 'they are' and that would not make sense in the sentence. The correct answer is B.
4	A	This sentence references something that will happen in the future. Answer choice A, "will build" makes the most sense and references something that will happen in the future.
5	D	With this sentence, we are looking for a word that will go along with "they" because the garden belongs to someone which tells us that we want to find a possessive word. The best answer choice is D, "their."
6	B	The answer choice that sounds the best is B, singing.
7	A	We are looking for a positive word that makes sense in the sentence. The best choice is A, "does."
8	D	Since Mickey's brother takes Mickey's toys we are looking for a pronoun to replace Mickey. The correct answer choice is D, "his."
9	C	The sentence is referencing a specific group of holiday lights. In this case, the best choice is C, "those."
10	D	The correct adverb to complete the sentence is "happily," answer D.

Demonstrate Command of Punctuation (L.6.2.A)

Question No.	Answer	Detailed Explanations
1	A	You must have quotations around what is said out loud. For that reason, answer choice A is correct.
2	C	Answer choice C is correct. There are two comma rules in place here. There needs to be a comma in items in a series (bananas, oranges, and cherries) and there is a compound sentence, so there needs to be a comma before the but.
3	A	Answer choice A is correct. There needs to be a semicolon after year because there are two complete sentences. You can't just put them together with a comma. It has to be a comma and a conjunction or a semicolon.
4	C	Answer choice C is correct. There has to be quotation marks around anything that is said out loud.
5	B	The only comma should be between the day and year. An apostrophe is used in Year's because year is a singular day.
6	C	The correct answer is C. The only comma that is needed is between the two clauses. "Which made my mom happy" is a dependent clause and the other clause is independent. It needs a conjunction or to be set apart in commas.
7	A	The correct answer is A. This is a compound sentence, so there needs to be a comma between vacation and but. Also, there needs to be a comma between the city and state (Dallas, Texas.)
8	D	There must always be a comma between the city and state. There should be a comma after Albany and a comma after Flourtown. Since the sentence is a question, it should end with a question mark rather than a period.
9	D	Answer choice D is correct because it's the only one where the You is capitalized. Any time a new sentence is used in dialogue, the first word in the sentence needs to be capitalized. There should also be an apostrophe in the contraction shouldn't.
10	C	Answer choice C is correct. There should be commas in the items in a series (pizza, grilled cheese, and tacos) and there should be a comma before but (because it's a compound sentence). There should also be an apostrophe in the word didn't because it is a contraction for the words did not.

Correct Spelling (L.6.2.B)

Question No.	Answer	Detailed Explanations
1	B	Answer choice B is correct because that is the correct spelling of the flour that you cook with. This type of flour is made from grinding wheat.
2	C	Answer choice C is the correct word for the type of flowers mentioned in the sentence. The other options do not make sense in the sentence.
3	B	Answer choice B is correct. Stair is the correct spelling as the word is used in the sentence. Option A is a homophone. Option C is another word for guiding.
4	B	Threw is the correct word to use in the above sentence. The others are homophones.
5	B	The first word is an adverb meaning "very," and the second word is an adjective meaning "not loud."
6	A	Answer choice A has the correct spelling of the word. Options C and D make sense but are not spelled correctly.
7	C	Answer choice C has the correct spelling of the word.
8	A	Answer choice A has the correct spelling of the word.
9	C	Answer choice C has the correct spelling of the word.
10	D	Answer choice D has the correct spelling of principal as it is used in the sentence. Option A is spelled correctly, but the definition does not make sense in the sentence.

Vary Sentences (L.6.3.A)

Question No.	Answer	Detailed Explanations
1	D	The sentences can be combined to make a compound sentence using the conjunction so. The correct answer is D.
2	A	The sentences can be combined to make a compound sentence using the conjunction but. The correct answer is A.
3	C	The sentences can best be combined by listing the different things that will be at the party using commas to separate items in a series.
4	A	The sentence fragment, after school, can be used as a dependent clause to make a complex sentence. The correct answer is A.
5	D	To keep the sentences from being repetitive, they can be combined together. Answer choice D makes the most sense.
6	C	Since the author likes both summer and spring but spring best, it is best to combine these sentences into a compound sentence using the contrasting conjunction but.
7	B	The sentence fragment can be turned into a dependent clause to create a complex sentence. The correct answer is B.
8	C	Since the author is listing things they have to do, combining each task and separating them with commas is the best way to combine these sentences. The correct answer is C.
9	A	Combining the two sentences into one simple sentence is the best option. The correct answer is A.
10	B	Using the adjective brown to describe the puppy and the list its other attributes creates the best sentence. The correct answer is B.

Maintain Consistency in Style and Tone (L.6.3.B)

Question No.	Answer	Detailed Explanations
1	A	While each sentence says basically the same thing, only the first sentence paints the clearest picture of what was actually happening. The correct answer is A.
2	B	While each sentence has the same meaning, sentence B uses the most descriptive words and style.
3	D	Each sentence adds just a little more detail to better explain the topic. Answer choice D is correct.
4	B	Answer choice A appears to be too choppy while answer choice C is too short. The best answer choice is B.
5	D	Sometimes fewer words, and more to the point is best. The correct answer choice is D.
6	C	Even though there are still 2 sentences, answer choice C maintains the best style and tone for the sentences.
7	A	Choices A and D are both possible; however, answer choice A offers a more varied and imaginative sentence style.
8	B	Answer choice B has the best overall style and tone of the four choices.
9	C	Answer choice C is the most concise while not using repetitive vocabulary.
10	C	Answer choice C uses the smoothest language while creating a picture of what is going on.

Use Context Clues to Determine Word Meaning (L.G.4.A)

Question No.	Answer	Detailed Explanations
1	B	Julio was happy, not disappointed, but the text tells us that he was also something else. Satisfied and pleased are very similar to happy, so they are not something else. He expected other boys to win the title, so the best use of context to figure out the word "astounded" is to select "very surprised."
2	C	The signal word "but" tells us that the opposite of flimsy is strong because spider silk is stronger than steel.
3	A	The text tells us what is on every side of New Jersey, so we know that bordered is the same thing as surrounded by.
4	A	Answer A is the answer that makes the most sense. Africa is large, so none of the other answers make sense.
5	A	Never leaving someone means that you are loyal. Answer choice A is correct.
6	C	Based on the sentence, beneficial means good for you. Doctors wouldn't tell you to do it unless it was good for you.
7	D	Because it was unbearable, we know that the smell was awful. The correct answer is D.
8	A	Because the celebrity was overwhelmed, we know there were a lot of questions. For that reason, the answer is A.
9	C	Because it was summer, we know that sweltering means hot. It would never be cold on a beach in the summer.
10	A	We know that it will be a word with a negative connotation and the only negative word that fits the sentence is A.

Use Common Roots and Affixes (L.6.4.B)

Question No.	Answer	Detailed Explanations
1	D	An affix can either be a prefix or a suffix, but a suffix will never be at the beginning of a word. Suffixes are only at the ends of words. The correct answer is D.
2	A	Incapable and not being able to do something are the same thing, so the only possible answer is A.
3	C	"-age" is the suffix that is the same in all three words. The correct answer is C.
4	B	"An-" is the only prefix that all three words have in common. The correct answer is B.
5	C	"Less" means "without," so the answer is C.
6	A	"-Ology" is the study of, so the answer is A. Although option D mentions study, -ology is not only the study of animals.
7	C	"Comm-" means "together," so C is the correct answer.
8	C	Both A and B are true, so the answer is C.
9	B	This is a two syllable word, so there should only be one hyphen between the n and the t. The answer is B.
10	D	Monarch only has two syllables, so it will only have one hyphen when you divide it. The hyphen should be between the two syllables, which is the case in answer choice D.

Consult Reference Materials (L.6.4.C)

Question No.	Answer	Detailed Explanations
1	B	Alphabetize means to rearrange the words in the order that they would appear in the dictionary. Answer choice B is the only one where the words are correctly alphabetized.
2	D	Alphabetize means to rearrange the words in the order that they would appear in the dictionary. Answer choice D is the only one where the words are alphabetized correctly.
3	D	Alphabetize means to rearrange the words in the order that they would appear in the dictionary. Answer choice D is the only one where the words are alphabetized correctly.
4	D	The dictionary contains all of these things, so answer choice D is true.
5	C	A synonym is what you find in the thesaurus. That is where you go when you're looking for a new word to replace an existing word.
6	B	Dictionaries are in alphabetical order, so answer choice B is correct.
7	D	Guidewords are at the top and guide you in your search for the word. They allow you to figure out if the word you are looking up falls within the guidewords for that page.
8	A	Organized is 3 syllables, so the answer is A.
9	C	Jacket is 2 syllables, so the answer is C.
10	B	It has 3 syllables, so answer choice B is correct.

Name: _____   Date: _____

Determine the Meaning of a Word (L.6.4.D)

Question No.	Answer	Detailed Explanations
1	B	Based upon the usage in the sentence, the word "misplaced" means to lose. The correct answer is B.
2	C	While the word "brisk" can mean both fast and cool, in this particular sentence it means "cool." The correct answer is C.
3	C	Since Natalie and Sophia are looking forward to their ride, the answer must have a positive connotation. The correct answer is "exciting," C.
4	D	Mundane means repetitive or boring. The correct answer choice is D. The context clues in the sentences help you determine this.
5	A	"Ravenous" means to be hungry. The correct answer is A. The context clues in the sentences help you determine this.
6	D	To triumph over someone or something means to win. The correct answer is D.
7	B	For something to be "bewitching" then it has captured your attention in a positive way. The correct answer is "charming," B.
8	D	Julia does not enjoy fishing, therefore it must be awful. The correct answer is D. The context clues in the sentences help you determine this.
9	A	In the context of the sentence, "perspective" means look or appearance. The correct answer is A.
10	D	A dictionary, thesaurus, and glossary can all give you an idea of what a word means. The correct answer is D, "All of the above."

Interpret Figures of Speech (L.6.5.A)

Question No.	Answer	Detailed Explanations
1	D	The sentence uses the repeated sound /j/ so it is an example of alliteration and a comparison using "like" so it is also an example of a simile.
2	A	The sentence does not mean to literally not spill the beans but rather not tell a secret. The correct answer is A, idiom.
3	B	The sentence is comparing a sandwich to a car using "as" which means it is a simile.
4	A	An extreme exaggeration is an example of hyperbole.
5	C	The sentence is giving human like characteristics to a bear. This is personification.
6	D	A word that represents its sound is onomatopoeia.
7	B	The sentence is comparing Katy to a pig without using "like" or "as." This is a metaphor.
8	B	An extreme exaggeration is an example of hyperbole.
9	A	"Stop pulling my leg" does not mean that someone is literally pulling one's leg. It means to stop teasing. This is an idiom.
10	B	The sentence compares Danielle's dancing to a swan using "as." It is a simile.

Use Relationships to better Understand Words (L.6.5.B)

Question No.	Answer	Detailed Explanations
1	A	The reason the flights were cancelled was the blizzard, so answer choice A is the only one that is correct.
2	B	The flood is what caused the people to be left homeless, so answer choice B is correct.
3	C	Pedro got the job because of his friendly attitude, so answer choice C is correct.
4	A	Answer choice A is correct because the only mammal listed is giraffe.
5	A	The only bird listed is a parrot, so A is correct.
6	B	The only dessert listed is pie, so B is the correct answer.
7	C	Answer choice C is the only one that puts things in the correct order.
8	B	Bees are the only insect listed, so answer choice B is correct.
9	B	The smoky smell was caused by the burned popcorn, so answer choice B is correct.
10	C	Answer choice C is the only one that shows the correct cause and effect.

Distinguish Between Word Associations and Definitions (L.6.5.C)

Question No.	Answer	Detailed Explanations
1	B	"Denotation" is the dictionary or literal meaning of a word. The correct answer is B.
2	C	"Connotation" refers to how the word makes us feel. The correct answer is C.
3	D	All the words listed have the same denotation as the word "house."
4	C	A child is often referred to as an adolescent. The correct answer is C.
5	C	Answer choices A and B, are structurally similar but the words have no similarities other than that. Answer choice D is opposites. Answer choice C is the correct answer.
6	D	Answer choice A and B are both antonyms so they do not have the same denotation. Horse and rabbits are similar in that they are both mammals but they do not have the same denotation. The correct answer is D.
7	D	The word "cheap" has a negative connotation to it.
8	B	The word "calamity" is not quite as hard as "disaster" therefore it has a positive connotation.
9	A	When thinking about something being messy, "filthy" is the answer choice that is the most negative.
10	C	A nice, or positive, way to say old is to say that someone is "elderly."

Use Grade Appropriate Words (L.6.6)

Question No.	Answer	Detailed Explanations
1	B	Answer choice B is an example of the word racket when it means noise.
2	D	In answer choice D, since the person has to bear weight or hold themselves up on their broken ankle, it is the correct answer.
3	C	If the little boy is being patient in line then he is quietly waiting. The correct answer is C.
4	B	Pounding on something until it breaks would be pounding to hit. The correct answer is B.
5	A	A pack or group of wolves mean that answer choice A is correct.
6	B	Since the author uses the words "even though they studied" it gives the impression that they did not feel too confident about their test. This would mean they felt anxious. The correct answer choice is B.
7	A	While the Grand Canyon is brown and stationary it is not small. The best word to describe it would be immense. The correct answer is A.
8	D	If a person needs to spend extra time training for a race then it probably is not easy or smooth. The correct answer choice is D, rigorous.
9	A	If Joey got caught cheating then he probably got himself into a predicament. The correct answer is A.
10	D	The best thing a team could be would be diligent about practicing. The correct answer choice is D.

Lumos StepUp™ is an educational app that helps students learn and master grade-level skills in Math and English Language Arts.

The list of features includes:

- Learn Anywhere, Anytime!

- Grades 3-8 Mathematics and English Language Arts

- Get instant access to the Common Core State Standards

- One full-length sample practice test in all Grades and Subjects

- Full-length Practice Tests, Partial Tests and Standards-based Tests

- 2 Test Modes: Normal mode and Learning mode

- Learning Mode gives the user a step-by-step explanation if the answer is wrong

- Access to Online Workbooks

- Provides ability to directly scan QR Codes

- And it's completely FREE!

http://lumoslearning.com/a/stepup-app

About Online Workbooks

- When you buy this book, 1 year access to online workbooks is included

- Access them anytime from a computer with an internet connection

- Adheres to the Common Core State Standards

- Includes progress reports

- Instant feedback and self-paced

- Ability to review incorrect answers

- Parents and Teachers can assist in student's learning by reviewing their areas of difficulty

INCLUDES Online Workbooks!

Course Name: Grade 4 Math Prep

Lesson Name:	Correct	Total	% Score	Incorrect
Introduction				
Diagnostic Test		3	0%	3
Number and Numerical Operations				
Workbook - Number Sense	2	10	20%	8
Workbook - Numerical Operations	2	25	8%	23
Workbook - Estimation	1	3	33%	2
Geometry and measurement				
Workbook - Geometric Properties		6	0%	6
Workbook - Transforming Shapes				
Workbook - Coordinate Geometry	1	3	33%	2
Workbook - Units of Measurement				
Workbook - Measuring Geometric Objects	3	10	30%	7
Patterns and algebra				
Workbook - Patterns	7	10	70%	3
Workbook - Functions and relationships				

LESSON NAME: Workbook - Geometric Properties

Elapsed Time: 01:19

Question No. 2

What type of motion is being modeled here?

Select right answer
- ◯ a translation
- ◯ a rotation 90° clockwise
- ◉ a rotation 90° counter-clockwise
- ◯ a reflection

[Previous question] [Next question]

Report Name: Missed Questions

Student Name: Lisa Colbright
Cours Name: Grade 4 Math Prep
Lesson Name: Diagnostic Test

The faces on a number cube are labeled with the numbers 1 through 6. What is the probability of rolling a number greater than 4?

Answer Explanation

(C) On a standard number cube, there are six possible outcomes. Of those outcomes, 2 of them are greater than 4. Thus, the probability of rolling a number greater than 4 is "2 out of 6" or 2/6.

A)		1/6
B)		1/3
C)	Correct Answer	2/6
D)		3/6

Made in the USA
Lexington, KY
06 February 2017